Ghosts of Boston Town

Ghosts of Boston Town

Three Centuries of True Hauntings

Holly Mascott Nadler

DOWN EAST BOOKS

ISBN 0-89272-535-4
Library of Congress Control Number 2002106574

Printed at Versa Press, E. Peoria, Ill.

2   4   5   3   1

Down East Books • Camden, Me.
Book orders: (800) 766-1670
www.downeastbooks.com

Cover photograph: Residence at corner of Dartmouth St. and
Commonwealth Ave., 1874. BOSTON PUBLIC LIBRARY PRINT DEPT.

IN LOVING MEMORY OF MY FATHER
LARRY MASCOTT
WHO, IN THE SPIRIT OF THIS BOOK, HAS MADE
A FEW POSTHUMOUS APPEARANCES HIMSELF

Contents

IV. Haunted Landmarks / 95

V. Haunted Outer 'Hoods / 129

VI. Haunted Environs / 157

Acknowledgments

With the endless research involved in a project of this nature, there is always a plethora of people to thank, from the friendly cop on the street corner who pointed me toward the haunted dorm, to the young man who left a message on my machine about that same dorm, only to be cut off mid-message, and who never returned my follow-up call. (Is he okay?!) But I absolutely must thank by name all the people who helped to connect me with what some might define as the ultimate "unconnectable": Dick Mason, manager of the Omni Parker House; ghost-hunter Jim McCabe, who guides Boston's haunted walking tours and who was so generous with his private stock of information; Anita Canzian, Julie Moynihan, Stuart Sigman, Troy Siegfried, Susan Landry, Mary Lee MacCormack, Jeff Breeze, Amy Santinello, and Bob Saftel, all of whom pointed me in the direction of delicious stories; and my sidekick, Margaret Maes, who helped me track down leads and who would be plucky enough to sashay up to a grizzly bear and ask him if he has any ghosts in his cave.

Copp's Hill Burial Ground, Hull Street, in the North End
Photographed c. 1890

Introduction

Boston *looks* haunted.

Stop on any corner in the old historic neighborhoods and focus your stare like a cinematographer framing a shot for a movie scene. Do you notice the way the old gaslight casts a silver haze over the dark stone walls of the Victorian townhouse? And what's that shimmering behind the heavy red velvet drapes? It's a lady in white, isn't it? But why is she standing so preternaturally still? Is she even…alive?

In all the country New England holds the richest repository of stories of the supernatural. And why not? The region has all the elements of a ghost factory. First, you take a foundation of Native American culture trampled underfoot, its burial grounds shoveled aside for Colonial farms, townships, and homes. From a rational point of view, this shouldn't matter one bit, but it does, it does. Too many authentic hauntings have originated over the site of a desecrated cemetery for researchers into the paranormal to overlook this vital connection. What is termed in the "para-business" an energy vortex begins to emerge, and what you get is a hatchery for ghosts. Add to that the layers of colorful history—ragtag militia vs. redcoats, Puritans vs. witches, pirates and smugglers vs. everyone, and haughty aristocrats, if not violently opposed, then discreetly resistant to ambitious immigrants. With all the murder, mayhem, and power grabs played out along the northeast seaboard, is it any wonder that Boston, the area's oldest, biggest, and—in its own uptight, repressed way—most passionate city should be overrun with spirits?

I came to writing about Boston ghosts by the circuitous route of London and Martha's Vineyard. In the early 1980s I flew to England to visit my parents, incurable world travelers who'd holed up for a season in a cozy, partially subterranean flat in the Kensington district. We attended a play a day—God bless those London theatre ticket prices!—and we became addicted to the city's vast roster of walking tours. My favorite was "The Ghosts of London." Even undertaken in the light of a warm June afternoon, that one managed to scare the cookies out of all three of us!

I returned to the Vineyard inspired to start my own line of walking tours. From the outset I knew "The Ghosts of Edgartown" would be the jewel in the crown of my tour menu. Sure enough, now many years later, I can still expect a crowd of twenty, thirty, or even forty-plus people waiting for me to come give them the creeps on any given summer night. The walk-and-talk about ghosts led me to write a book about Vineyard spooks, and in 1994 Down East Books brought out *Haunted Island.* I recently received a call from a nice manager at Bunch of Grapes, the Vineyard's year-round bookstore, to tell me that *Haunted Island* is their second biggest seller of all time. I share this information not so much to brag, but to point out how fascinated by ghosts we all seem to be.

In any event, for those Vineyarders who require a regular dose of metropolitan delights, Boston is our mecca. Once we've ferried over the seven miles of water that separate us from the mainland, we're only a ninety-minute drive from town. I stay at a favorite B&B on Beacon Hill—that timeless stage-set for an Edith Wharton novel—and it was there that I frequently found myself thinking about Boston ghosts.

You see, I'm a bit of a ghost feeler (so was Edith Wharton, as you'll discover in Chapter 8), officially known as a clairsentient. The most fully realized psychics are those who can *see* ghosts. Those of us who only feel them face a rockier road because, without always knowing why, we're in a fairly regular state of mild-to-extreme anxiety. My first experience of this occurred at age six, when my Brownie troop enrolled in swim lessons. Although I'd always been a contented pond bather and puddle splasher and a happy camper around neighbors' pools, I froze at the edge of this municipal pool into which my sister Brownies had already gleefully leapt. I was paralyzed with fear, and when our troop leader tried to coax me into the water, I burst into big, wracking sobs. My next memory is of being hauled back into my clothes in the locker room, thrust into a station wagon, and returned to my mother, a Brownie reject if there ever was one.

Once I left the vicinity of the pool I was back to my chirpy young self. Eventually we got our own pool, and the woman hired to teach me to swim met with no quakes or shakes on my part. A year or so later I learned that a nine-year-old boy had drowned in that municipal pool not too long before my inauspicious first swim lesson.

But this encounter with pool anxiety wasn't just a one-shot deal. Every so often I stand beside a pool that really disturbs me—simply *freaks me out!* That first excruciating—and humiliating—experience with my "condition" inspired me to search for answers. On the rare subsequent occasions when this feeling of dread has come over me, I've investigated the biography of the pool in question, and in every case I've discovered that within recent memory someone had indeed drowned in those deceptively clear aqua waters.

Thank God the sensation is more subdued when I intercept spirit life on land. If I reacted to every psychic imprint the way I do a pool-related death, I'd have been locked up in the proverbial padded cell a long time ago. Instead, what I feel in many locations is a vague unease, an unmistakable "wimp factor." If a house is haunted, I'll sense which room is primarily implicated. At one point I lived in a duplex where the dining room unsettled me, though it would have taken a high-test ghost seer to determine what precisely lurked within the room's innocuous walls of pink floral wallpaper and white wainscoting. I avoided the dining room when I was alone in the house, though with friends seated around the table at night by candlelight you would never have mistaken it for a chamber of horrors.

With this predilection for sensing ghosts, my jaunts around Boston have always kept me looking over my shoulder and staring up at buildings to savor the quaint juxtapositions of antique elements, so much of it evocative of old Bela Lugosi movies. You can imagine the shadow of an Edwardian gentleman in frock coat and top hat lengthening over a brick sidewalk, and you take it in stride; it's part of the *phyllo* dough of Boston's myriad layers of history, intrigue, art, and melodrama, all of it wrapped up in a nearly transparent top glaze of Boston Brahmin elegance.

Of course it was a different matter altogether when I began to collect the ghost stories that make up this book. As the saying goes, what you are about to hear is true: I've changed some of the names and adapted some of the circumstances at the subjects' request, but as far as this "ghost-feeler" and researcher of the paranormal can tell, the following accounts are factual, and some of them are darn scary, especially because they truly happened.

But I'll let you be the judge of the degree of scariness, intrepid reader. We'll see if *your* "wimp factor" is less easily triggered than mine ...

PART I

In-Town Ghosts

Tremont Street, looking toward Park Street Church, 1860

It's been said

*that you could plunk Benjamin Franklin or
Paul Revere into the heart of Boston without a map
today, and he would know his way around town.
The streets haven't changed, although the
old legend about paving the original cow paths
is considered a bit of a stretch.
It's more likely that the early dwellers
had no pressing desire to line up their streets
in a neurotic, up-and-down, side-to-side grid.
What's wrong, after all, with curving around this
park over here and keeping the quaint angles
of this five-way intersection? Maybe it's knowledge
of the familiar lay of the land that enables
so many Boston spirits to filter through the
gauze of time without undue effort.* ⇥

⇥ 1 ⇤

The Tainted Honeymoon

I should have stopped to ask myself why an apartment on Beacon Hill would rent so cheaply," says Jim Mackey, looking back to his harrowing experience in the late 1990s in a garret on Pinckney Street. On a blue and gold day in September, Jim had arrived to check out the apartment, and even before he entered the charming old brownstone he was captivated by Pinckney's bay windows, cobbled brick sidewalks, ornate wooden doors, and flowerpots overflowing with geraniums, primroses, and Shasta daisies. A female friend from college days at Cornell had recently relinquished the Pinckney lease and advised Jim to contact the landlady. Jim says, "My friend did joke in passing about a ghost, but hey, who was I to be picky about a five-hundred-dollar-a-month-rental? Besides, I didn't believe in ghosts, and if I encountered one after all, bring it on! How much could a little bit of supernatural fluff hurt a big tough guy like me? That was my attitude."

The landlady was a morose woman in her sixties, with faded blond hair and mousy features. She didn't smile once when she showed Jim the apartment on the top floor, but that hardly deterred him. The woman's quarters on the lower three floors were sealed off from the central staircase, so there would be little likelihood of crossing paths with her. The rental unit was small but sweetly evocative of another age, with mahogany moldings, skylights, custom shelves, worn but charming antique furniture, and French doors opening onto a balcony with a distant view of the river. The ambiance was a bit feminine for Jim's taste, but he figured that would come in handy for romancing future girlfriends.

On the day Jim moved in, he called his friend from Cornell and asked what she wanted him to do with the dresses she'd left behind in the bedroom closet. "Those aren't mine," she giggled. "I'm strictly an L.L. Bean kinda gal. Those dresses come with the rental."

"Well, they're not my size," he said facetiously.

"So, go on a diet."

"Maybe I should box 'em up and give them to the landlady?"

"I wouldn't," replied his friend, her tone suddenly guarded. "The ghost doesn't like you to change anything."

"Get real!" Jim scoffed. When he hung up, he marched over to the closet with the intention of yanking the gowns from their hangers and plopping them into a plastic bag. But then, peering at the garments more closely, he reconsidered. Six or seven in all, they were perfect specimens of fifties sheath dresses, a bit moth-eaten and stained, but of high quality linen in shades of tan, beige, and black, with one pink number that reminded him of Jackie Kennedy. Something about the dresses made him more respectful of their pride of place in the closet, and he decided to leave them undisturbed until his own wardrobe grew enough to fill the space. He was just starting out as an associate at a prestigious law firm, and he knew that over the next few seasons he'd be investing in new suits. "I thought that with any luck, by the time I needed a bigger closet, I would have advanced enough in my field to afford an apartment upgrade. This was a cute place, but it reminded me of being a struggling artist—not my personality at all."

The first night alone in the apartment, he woke a little after two in the morning as a stiff, cold breeze wafted over his face. "I thought I'd closed all the windows, but I turned on the light to double-check. Sure enough the bedroom windows were tightly shut, and I didn't see how a brisk wind could have made it all the way down the hallway, hooking a left inside the bedroom to knock me awake." He nestled back into the pillow, and just as he started to doze again, he heard a series of low moans emanating from the closet. He remembered his friend's remarks about a ghost, but the thought, rather than frightening him, made him chuckle. He decided that no unexplained breezes and closet vocalizations would keep him from a good night's rest.

Over the next few weeks Jim was occasionally awakened by the cold wind and the moans from the closet, but as before, he paid little attention to them. "It made for interesting small talk around the water cooler," he says. Other signs of an invisible roommate began to surface. Some mornings Jim would lumber out to the tiny living space to find the dirty dishes he'd left in the sink the night before now cleaned and neatly stacked on the counter dish rack. Also, the chrysanthemums and hollies in pots out on the balcony never seemed to require watering, even though they were shielded from rain by an overhang. "I told myself I'd water them if they ever looked droopy, but they never did, so I figured it was another chore the ghost took care of. I knew a good thing when I saw it. I just wished my invisible roommate could fold my socks and bake lasagna."

Jim's experiences with the entity weren't always so tolerable. One night he woke up, and instead of moans, he heard a woman weeping inside the closet. The lamentation sounded so real that he felt the urge to get up and investigate, but for the first time he grew anxious. He was aware of his mood rapidly deteriorating until he felt saturated by sorrow, as deeply upset as was the presence that wept beneath the vintage gowns. "I'm an even-keeled guy, and this was my first experience with depression. It only lasted a few minutes, thank God. The sobs wound down, and I fell asleep. The next morning, I was more or less back to normal, but I felt a bit shaken, so as soon as I was showered and dressed, I padded downstairs and knocked on my landlady's door."

He bluntly asked her, "What's up with the ghost in my apartment?"

She looked chagrined at first, but then her usual aloof expression reasserted itself. "I don't know what you're talking about."

He tried to furnish details, but she interrupted him, "I have to fold some towels." She shut the door in his face.

Jim placed another call to his former college pal, and this time he was grumpy: "Okay, what do you know about this?"

It turned out his friend hadn't experienced anywhere near the amount of disturbances to which Jim had been subjected. Her contact was restricted to the occasional cold breeze and articles in the front room being moved around. "She never did my dishes for me," his friend said. "She must be in love with you; I guess there's no accounting for taste in ghosts."

Jim's friend had also tried to quiz the landlady but had learned nothing until she happened to run into the woman's daughter, visiting from Portland, Maine. From the younger woman she found out that in 1954, a girl named Abby had rented the garret quarters from an earlier owner and had subsequently been devastated by a failed love affair. She committed suicide by slitting her wrists in the bathtub.

"But there's only a shower stall," said Jim, relieved to think that the story must be fiction.

"Duh!" replied his friend. "No one wanted to live with the Death Tub. They had it replaced."

Jim began to think about moving. The mysterious and sudden stab of depression had bothered him more than he would have thought possible. He made up his mind that if he fell victim to it again, he would pack a bag and book himself into a hotel, pronto. But soon a major event occurred in his life that took his mind off his own personal ghost and every other aspect of daily living: he fell in love.

Jody was the newest paralegal in the firm. Pretty, blond, blue-eyed Jody had grown up in Columbus, Ohio, and for Jim she seemed to have stepped out of a 1930s screwball comedy. "She was so wholesome and sweet, and supportive, and positive. There wasn't a sarcastic bone in her body. She was totally different from all the other girls I'd met who were so intent on being cool." On the first date, Jim fell head over heels in love with the lovely Ohioan, and the feeling was reciprocated. "We were caught up in the fantasy of love at first sight. I took her down to my parents' empty cottage on the Cape that weekend and proposed to her on a windy night on the beach. We decided to return to the Cape the very next weekend and get married by a Sandwich justice of the peace. It was madness, but fantastic madness."

In the coming week, Jim invited Jody to dinner at his apartment, warning her ahead of time about the ghost. "After we married, our plan was for me to move into Jody's apartment in the Back Bay area. It was larger and just basically more grown-up, but I wanted my fiancée to see how and where I lived before we blended our lives."

Jim had picked up some lemon chicken, grilled vegetables, and sesame noodles from a gourmet shop on Charles Street, and by candlelight he laid out a romantic spread on the granite table on the balcony. Jody expressed her delight over the old-fashioned apartment, and during dinner she said, "I feel as if we've stepped back into a Henry James novel. Maybe we should live here."

The minute the words were out, the iron-and-glass-framed door to the balcony slammed shut with a force that made Jim gasp and Jody scream. "Was that your ghost?" she asked, her face deathly pale.

Jim looked at the ivy-covered backs of the buildings opposite them. There wasn't a breath of wind in the night air. Exasperated, he said, "Abby, knock it off!"

They retired to the tiny dining alcove for a dessert of piña colada sorbet. Once inside, Jody grew uncharacteristically testy. "I'm not really a dessert eater. You might as well know that about me," she groused, leaving her bowl untouched. She made some peevish comments about the rusty stove and the useless-looking refrigerator. "I'd better be going. I'm not really comfortable here," she confided.

Jim walked Jody to the sidewalk, where her mood dramatically brightened. He was so relieved to have his good-natured fiancée restored to him that, rather than bundling her into a cab, he walked her home the twenty-or-so blocks to Marlborough Street.

He stared up at the modern brick building. "It will be better living here," he said.

"Much," she concurred, and they kissed goodnight.

The following weekend, the elopement took place without a hitch. Jim splurged and rented a Mercedes convertible for the ride to Sandwich. Their paperwork completed, they were married in a high-windowed room of the Colonial-style town hall. Afterward, they strolled to a seaside bed-and-breakfast and stepped into their water-view room with a canopied bed and a fireplace. "Where's that draft coming from?" asked Jody in a peevish voice he'd only heard once before from her—the time she'd visited his apartment. Jim glanced around at the closed French doors, and all of a sudden he was reminded of the improbably cold and brisk wind that routinely swept into his bedroom on Pinckney Street.

Inwardly he groaned, "Abby, if you've come along on my honeymoon, I'm going to kill you!" And then he laughed at the oxymoron of killing a ghost.

More traumatic than any visit from the Other Side, however, was the disintegration of Jody's normally sunny personality. Jim felt as if he'd fallen in love with one woman, then taken her evil twin on their honeymoon. Nothing about the inn pleased her. "It's so shabby. I can smell the mold. My allergies are flaring up! I saw a bug in the bathroom! This is unacceptable!" Her pretty face, which to Jim had seemed so kind and corn-fed pretty, now housed narrow, mean little blue eyes, a nose red and runny from allergies, and a mouth wrenched down at the corners in constant disapproval.

They went for a walk on the sound, and even that sublime body of water annoyed her: "We should have found an inn on the ocean side in Truro or Chatham. I like waves better than this stupid bathtub."

Before leaving the city, Jim had asked around to find the most romantic restaurant in the Sandwich area. Not surprisingly, Jody hated that as well. Her lobster bisque wasn't warm enough and lacked a sufficient complement of lobster. Her grilled vegetables had absorbed too much oil, and her swordfish was dry and overcooked.

At last, Jim threw down his napkin and demanded, "What's going on with you? Do you regret being married, because believe me, I regret it more and more with every passing moment."

The ensuing argument will be left to the private scrapbooks of Jim and Jody's memories. The upshot was that they returned to Boston that very night and parted company to sleep in their own apartments. Come morning, Jim inveigled a colleague in his law firm to start work on an annulment.

Jody, for her part, called in her resignation and never again set foot in Jim's firm. Jim also made a substantial change in his life: he returned to his apartment with two buddies and a collection of moving boxes. He slipped the key in his landlady's door with a note advising her to rent only to women: "You've got a lonely ghost up there who's hell on a guy's love life," he added.

So, had Abby tagged along on his honeymoon and wrecked his chances for happiness with Jody? Some years after the incident—and still single—Jim has no definite answers. "The rational part of me thinks Jody just freaked at marrying a stranger and acted that way out of fear. Or maybe she was, bottom line, a nasty person, and once she 'got' me she let her true colors show. Or maybe she was mentally ill. There's never been any contact subsequent to our unholy honeymoon. But what I truly believe in my heart is that Abby had some kind of a ghostly crush on me, could detect that Jody wasn't all that nice, and somehow forced my 'bride' to reveal herself sooner rather than later. I actually feel grateful to the ghost. Imagine if it had taken me years to find out I'd married a selfish, whiny little twit. There'd have been no wriggling out of it with a lickety-split annulment."

$\rightleftharpoons$ 2 $\rightleftharpoons$

The Imaginary Friend

Rick and Claudia O'Brien and their three-year-old, Hudson, moved into a two-bedroom flat on Tileston Street in Boston's North End. Claudia's ancestors had emigrated from Sicily, Rick's from western Ireland, but both loved the neighborhood's tiny Italian groceries, the bistros fragrant with basil, oregano, and garlic, the antique cobbled squares, and the parish church where the hours tolled from an old bell tower.

The apartment was paneled with time-darkened wood, but Claudia gained permission from the owner to paint the walls a pale shade called "buttercream," and that went a long way to brighten the otherwise shadowy rooms.

"We wanted to spruce up the kitchen and bathroom," said Claudia, "but that would have to wait until our economic situation improved." Rick managed a computer store on Commonwealth Avenue, and Claudia had started a small day care service to enable her to remain home with Hudson.

The day care was another issue the O'Briens had needed to clear with their landlady, Mrs. DiLullio, an eighty-seven-year-old widow who only recently had vacated her apartment to seek assisted living in the suburbs of Andover. "I went to visit her a couple of times," said Claudia, "and she really missed the

North End. She'd come to America at the age of thirteen to live with a family of cousins who spoke only English. She kept up her Italian by conversing with all the shopkeepers and older *paesani* in the neighborhood. She would have given anything to return to Tileston Street, but she'd broken her femur, and it didn't look as if she'd ever be able again to climb stairs or even walk without the greatest difficulty."

Mrs. DiLullio wore a pained expression on a massively lined face, white hair surrounding her head like a clump of cotton batting. Claudia had the impression the elderly woman had grown clinically depressed from the broken leg and the forced exile from her home and neighborhood.

"I once had a talk with her son about her condition, and he said his mother's doctor had her on an antidepressant, but as far as I could see, it wasn't helping. The only thing that could have cheered her up was watching the *passagiata* from a lawn chair on the sidewalk below her apartment."

One foggy night in October, all three O'Briens were fast asleep, Hudson in his tiny room next to his parents' slightly larger one. Suddenly, Rick and Claudia were awakened by their 100-watt overhead light flashing on. At the same time, all three of the apartment's smoke detectors began to blare. Rick's first instinct was to glance at the digital alarm clock: 3:18 a.m. He sniffed for smoke, but neither he nor Claudia could find any other hint of a fire.

Claudia ran to Hudson's room to find her son fast asleep, undisturbed by the drilling fire alarms, though his overhead light had also switched on. Rick ran to the front door, slid out the bolt, and flung the door wide to check for smoke in the hall and stairwell. No sign of a fire.

Once Rick and Claudia determined there was no danger of toasting to a crisp, they realized that every room in the apartment, including the kitchen and bathroom, glowed white from the 100-watt overhead bulbs they rarely used. But the relentlessly bleating alarms were a more serious problem. Anxiously, Rick mounted a stepladder and disassembled the living room detector, wrenching out the connection and yanking the battery. The two bedroom detectors continued to blare, and it wasn't until the third unit was disemboweled that silence returned to the apartment. The couple then switched off the annoying overhead lights and returned to bed, sleeping fitfully until dawn.

The following afternoon, Claudia received a call from Mrs. DiLullio's son: his mother had died in the assisted care residence at 3:18 that morning.

The next evening, Claudia was feeding Hudson in the kitchen when she heard the sound of the front door slamming. "We're in here!" she called, waiting for Rick to swoop in, plop his backpack on the counter, and kiss her on the forehead. When, after a minute, he failed to appear, Claudia said to Hudson, "Where did Daddy go?" She took a quick peek into the other rooms, and then decided Rick must have trudged back downstairs to check the mail. Or something. At that minute, the phone rang. It was Rick calling from the office. "Running late, baby. I'll be home in an hour."

Within days following Mrs. DiLullio's death, it was clear to the O'Briens that their apartment was now, in Rick's words, "fiendishly haunted." Until Rick had the bright idea of taking out the bulbs, the overhead lights flicked on almost every night. Rick kept all three smoke detectors disconnected and gutted; he knew that otherwise they would endure a regular serenade. Objects were mysteriously moved around, most notably their sizable futon sofa, which normally took center stage in the living room; every few days it ended up crammed against the wall in the dining ell.

Claudia had a theory: "I think Mrs. DiLullio missed her old furniture. According to her son, she'd had the place stuffed with heavy baroque Italian pieces. When he put the apartment up for rent, none of the prospective tenants wanted to live with that kind of furniture, so he stuck it in storage. Then Rick and I come along, paint the walls buttercream, and fill the space with stuff from Ikea and Target. It must've driven her crazy!"

The couple tried to laugh off the disturbances, but Claudia found herself increasingly on edge. "I would lie awake at night waiting for those stupid lights to flash on or for any new sign of something-not-right. And then I'd get to worrying about Hudson, next door. I'd imagine terrible things like a dark shape looming over his bed." The O'Briens discussed the possibility of bringing Hudson into their room but hesitated to signal their fear to him.

"I read a few books on the paranormal," said Claudia, "and I learned that some spirits require a certain length of time before moving on to the next world. We decided to give it a few more weeks to see if things quieted down. In the meantime, feeling like a total idiot, I'd talk out loud to Mrs. DiLullio, assuring her I was taking good care of her apartment and begging her to travel into the Light!"

Rick said, "The only light she seemed interested in was our hundred-watt bulbs."

One day Claudia sat on her living room floor with her six day care charges, all of them engaged in creating a group mural with crayons and a long roll of paper. A three-year-old named Sean, with a tow head and chipmunk cheeks, looked up from his work. "Where's Prima today?" he asked.

Claudia looked at him with a start. Prima was Mrs. Di-Lullio's first name.

But then with a flash of reason, Claudia assured herself that, unusual as that name might be, Sean undoubtedly had a young friend called Prima, perhaps named for a beloved grandma. "Is that a pal of yours?" she asked.

"She's an old lady who comes here to play with me."

"Where does Prima live?" asked Claudia.

He pointed in a downward direction. "Under the grass."

Claudia caught her breath. "And what does Prima look like?"

"She's very white," he said brightly. "White hair. White skin." He rummaged in the box of crayons with his tiny fingers until he found one called "Alabaster." Holding it up with a flourish, he said, "Like this."

Claudia tried to keep her nerves from fraying for the rest of the day, but she was relieved at five o'clock when all of her charges had been picked up by their parents. Earlier, she'd phoned one of the moms at work and asked if she'd take Hudson home with her for a suppertime play date. Now, all alone in the haunted apartment, Claudia arranged a circle of candles on the living room floor and plunked herself down in the middle of them. She'd heard that sage was used in shamanic practices as a purifying herb, so she dumped a jar of dried sage onto a heavy plate and ignited it into a gentle smolder. And then she began, between praying and chanting, to implore Prima DiLullio to quit the apartment once and for all.

Did the informal exorcism work?

The O'Briens claim mixed results. The more obstreperous forms of haunting ceased altogether—no more lights switching on or furniture being moved, and none of the kids ever again mentioned an imaginary elderly playmate. But Claudia was left with the sense that Mrs. DiLullio was keeping a low profile until a future time when a new set of tenants might be induced to live with a full-blown ghost.

"I know she's still hanging around," said Claudia. "Sometimes I smell lilacs in the air, and we don't have a single lilac-scented product. I'll be missing something one day and have it turn up exactly where I'd searched for it the day before. But at this point I think she's watching over us more than trying to freak us out. Recently, I found Hudson's window open every morning, even though we locked it each night. This got me to thinking, so I bought one of those air-testing monitors. Sure enough, when we plugged it into a wall socket in Hudson's room, it measured a small amount of carbon monoxide coming out of a faulty furnace. We got an engineer in immediately to take care of the problem. After that, no invisible being opened Hudson's window in the night—a good thing, what with winter just around the corner!"

Now that the O'Briens' ghost has been elevated from unwelcome phantom to guardian angel, Claudia and Rick have no immediate plans to move. "We love the North End," affirms Claudia, and Rick adds jokingly, "When our time comes, we'll probably want to be North End ghosts ourselves one day!"

❧ 3 ❧

The Hampshire Street Horror

"Greg and I were both in grad school—he at Harvard, I at B.U.—so we jumped at the chance to take a sublet on Hampshire Street in Cambridge," said Claire Cressy in relating her own true ghost story. "We loved Cambridge for its arty movie houses and ethnic restaurants. And there's all that great old architecture, but it's built lower. . . . A young doctor was renting out the ground-floor of a duplex. His place was *tres* grad-schoolish—big, shabby rooms with scuffed wood floors and scant furnishings—sort of sixties Danish with a few framed Miro and Kandinsky lithographs."

Claire and Greg met the original leaseholder only one time, just long enough to be shown around and receive the key. He was off to India for a year on a government medical aid program. "He was a little aloof, the kind of guy who has never found much use for charm." Claire said. "He was civil enough, but he never said anything about the entity living in his rooms. Either it never appeared to him, or he miraculously avoided its notice, or he was only pretending to be mellow, because any normal person would be a nervous wreck after living with that thing."

On the November day the young couple was to move in,

Greg borrowed a small flatbed truck to transport their belongings—about a dozen cardboard boxes, a TV set, and cat paraphernalia. "We'd been students so long," said Claire, "that we'd learned to travel light." When their meager pile of worldly goods was safely stashed inside the apartment, Claire picked up the blue plastic box containing their thirty-pound black-and-white cat, Reggie, and hefted it into the small foyer off the living room. The minute she set the box on the floor, a low growl issued from inside. Claire chuckled at the thought that perhaps they'd moved old Reg one too many times, though he'd never before been averse to a new setting. The couple had even traveled with the chubby feline for three months in Europe. "Every night we stayed in a different inn, and if our room was on the ground floor, we'd open the window to let Reggie out for a nocturnal romp. He always returned in the early morning, looking considerably the worse for wear, and he'd sleep like a dead thing in the car the next day. If cats could talk, Reggie would tell us all about his own completely separate European vacation."

But now the fat fur boy was showing signs of severe agoraphobia. Claire swung open the door to the cage, but Reggie refused to budge. She got down on her hands and knees and peered inside. Her normally lovable pet drew back his lips to expose sharp teeth and hissed at her. Claire blinked and drew away. Then she shrugged and went off to help Greg sort through the boxes.

An hour later, Claire remembered Reggie and bent down to peek in the box. He was still huddled inside, though this time he didn't hiss. Instead, he stared out with wide yellow eyes. She was tempted to drag him out, but he was acting so strangely, she was afraid he might bite or scratch her. Recalling his European adventure—his ability to stay out all night and find his way back—she dragged the box to the front door and pointed the big cat toward the fresh air of Hampshire Street.

A bolt of black and white fur shot out of the cage like a soft cannonball.

Reggie went missing for three days.

"We put up signs around the neighborhood and called our old digs clear across town, thinking Reggie might have made his way back there." Finally, on the third day, Greg spied something moving under the concrete steps of his apartment when he returned from a trip to the corner store. Crouching down to investigate, he spied Reggie: sullen, several pounds lighter, and covered with cobwebs. The couple decided to give the pet time to adjust. They let him stay outside, and they took to sliding his bowl of food under the steps. When he still refused to enter the apartment after a week, they gave up trying and boarded him with a friend in the Porter Square area. "Reggie took to the friend's apartment with his usual king-of-the-hill aplomb. You'd never have known he'd wimped out in our new home."

About a week and a half later, Greg and Claire got a taste of what had driven their cat to run for cover. A little past eleven o'clock on a chill November night, they returned from a potluck dinner. A light fog created an unworldly glow around the street lamps. The street seemed entirely deserted, every inhabitant of that cranny of Cambridge already in bed. Greg stuck the key in the front door lock, and immediately a shrill scream unfurled at them.

"It was a scream of rage—high-pitched, female, seeming to gush out of the lock," said Claire, "as if the door itself were outraged that we'd try to enter."

They shrunk back from the sound, and it stopped abruptly. The couple stared at one another in a wordless question: What should we do? Finally, Greg shrugged, turned the key in the lock and pushed open the door. No new screams issued forth. "We turned on every light, creeping our way from room to room. Finally, when we got ready for bed, Greg offered to go around and turn off all the lights. I told him, 'Don't you dare!'"

In the next few weeks, their work loads took their minds off their screaming doorknob, and in that same period nothing out of the ordinary reminded them of the troubling night when they'd slept with every light ablaze. And then, just before Christmas, as Claire returned from class on a blustery afternoon, she turned the key in the lock and the ear-splitting scream blasted out at her again. She shrank back and then skedaddled to the corner market, where she used a pay phone to reach Greg at his office. She found out when he planned on coming home, then sat in a nearby coffee shop waiting for her husband to brave the front door with her. They met at the appointed time outside the duplex, and Greg gingerly poked the key in the lock. They heard a reassuring clicking sound, uninterrupted by any unworldly howls. Claire sighed and Greg shrugged.

"After that, we tolerated the occasional shrieking lock. There was no set pattern to it. We half convinced ourselves there was some technical explanation having to do with rust and water pipes."

In January, Claire's nineteen-year-old cousin, Gillian, came to live with them until a lease became available in a bay-front apartment building in Revere. "She was taking a few classes at Lesley College and working in a book store, just sort of waiting to see what fresh vistas opened up to her. We gave her the back bedroom, and she was very grateful for the free rent—so grateful, in fact, it took her three weeks to tell us she was being terrorized each night."

Claire noticed that her cousin had started to act distant and uncommunicative. She worried that her guest might be prey to depression. Before gently broaching the subject, she checked with a relative, another cousin who'd spent more time with Gillian, to see if the young woman had any record of mood swings. "Gillian?" said the cousin with a chuckle. "You've got to be kidding! She's so sunny, people meeting her think she's on drugs."

All the same, Claire was concerned, so over the breakfast table one morning, she gently asked Gillian if something was bothering her. "She looked aghast at first, but then it all came rushing out: Every night as she lay in her bed, this terrible series of screams poured out of her closet. She was sure we heard it and couldn't understand why neither Greg nor I spoke of it. The poor kid had pushed her bed into a bay of windows at the opposite end of the room. She'd tacked a couple of nails in the ceiling so she could sling a blanket over the foot of the bed to give herself a shield from the thing in the closet."

After that discussion, Claire made up a bed for Gillian in Greg's den at the front of the house, off the living room. The three occupants of the duplex kept the door shut to the back bedroom, and if screams still raged from the closet, no one heard them. They thought they might have the problem licked. Even the front door knob seemed to have given up its infrequent banshee wail.

One night in February, Claire found herself alone in the apartment. Gillian had moved on to Revere, and Greg was in New Hampshire to give his mother moral support through knee surgery. "I must confess I was already predisposed to be nervous," Claire said. "When bedtime rolled around, I made a decision to keep all the lights on. I even turned on the TV set, though I hadn't watched it in at least two months. I brushed my teeth in the kitchen sink rather than traipse down the long hallway to the bathroom, which was adjacent to the infamous back bedroom. Then when it came time to hop into bed, I just stripped off my shoes and jeans and slept in the tee and plaid shirt I'd worn all day."

She tried to drowse off with the bedside lamp turned on, but it was no use: she needed darkness to get to sleep. With a last glance around the room to assure herself there were no phantoms lurking behind drapes or dressers, she switched off the lamp, then burrowed deeply under the covers. "I left my nose and forehead exposed, and that was it."

She slept for a while, then all at once she woke with a small gasp. A fragment of nightmare lodged in her brain at the moment of waking—she'd been dreaming of a disembodied head on the pillow next to hers. In the dream she'd turned to look, and she beheld an old woman's face, half of it melting away, drooping into decomposition. As she gazed in horror, the good eye of the face had opened and stared back at her. This last bit jolted her awake.

"And then I realized I'd awakened into an atmosphere far worse than the dream. There was something in the room. It was massing into a gray column at the foot of the bed, as if gathering strength to attack me in one fell swoop. I tried to move, but I was paralyzed. I tried to speak, but only a pitiful whimper came out of my throat. And I just knew that this thing hovering over me was pure evil, and that it wanted to deprive me off every last bit of my precious human energy. I'd heard of psychic vampires, but I'd never believed in them. Now I know that one had come for me that night!"

In the end, Claire was rescued by her rage. The rage built in her system, gathering strength and eventually forcing itself through her paralyzed body and vocal chords.

"Get out!" she shouted at the gray funnel of demonic energy. "You have no right here," she shouted. "Get out. Get out!" The power of her words broke through her deadened muscles, and she shot up in bed to switch on the lamp.

"For about four or five seconds the light picked up the shape. It was a figure cloaked in some kind of monk's robe. There was just a blur of a face, but its huge hands were lifted up, palms inward, the way surgeons raise their gloves. And then it faded away in front of my eyes."

Claire never tried to catch even another second of sleep in that apartment. She got up and dressed and took a taxi to South Station, where she dozed on a bench until the early bus for New Hampshire left in the first light of day. "Greg and I started making calls from his mother's house to line up a new apartment. I wouldn't even set foot back in Boston until I knew for certain I had a new roof over my head."

The couple returned in daylight to gather their belongings from the haunted duplex. "The young doctor who'd sublet to us had given us an address in Berkeley for sending our rent money. I think his sister or someone had been depositing it in a local bank for him. I dropped him a line to tell him we'd terminated our deal based on the paranormal activity in the apartment, of which I wished we'd been forewarned. I expected a fight from him—maybe even an attorney's letter—but we never heard from the guy, which leads me to believe he'd known all along. Hey, maybe that's why he thought he had to go all the way to India—to get away from that thing."

Claire and Greg, happily reunited with Reggie, moved to a sunny apartment in Somerville. When occasionally they speak of the haunting on Hampshire Street, they're invariably asked if they learned what circumstances may have led to the disturbances. Claire can only speculate, but she strongly suspects an initial event triggered a later aura of disaster. "Something awful must have happened in that back bedroom. Perhaps someone was murdered there or simply died alone and miserable. I think unhappy ghosts attract sinister energy. That demonic entity that terrorized me in my room clearly felt right at home in that sad old duplex. Next time we'll follow Reggie's cue: if he doesn't like a place, we'll book it out of there."

Amen. Maybe more of us should follow the lead of our pets.

⇥ 4 ⇤

Holy Water for an Unholy Being

To call the building a fixer-upper would be a supreme act of courtesy. You might as well call a half-incinerated '56 Chevy a classic in the making. But Lucia and Meryl Carruthers, sisters in their late fifties, one widowed, one divorced, decided to buy the shabby three-floor storefront in Back Bay. "We knew we had to be in that neighborhood," said Lucia. "To us, it's the most chic, the 'citiest' part of the city, what with all the shops on Newbury Street, and the little French bistros and fancy hotels. For two farm girls from Wisconsin, this was heaven."

The price of the building was cheap enough to leave them a goodly sum for renovating the three floors. They planned to use the ground floor for a combination bookstore and tea room. They would go on renting the second floor to the current leaseholder, a shiatsu masseuse. The third floor would serve as their residence, and it was this top story that caused them the most consternation.

The prior owners had operated the downstairs as a beauty parlor, and years before had painted the top-floor living quarters in various somber shades. The living room was a peeling midnight blue, the dining room an ancient maroon, and the three bedrooms a molding brown, ragged tan, and dilapidated forest green. Window sashes had rotted out, vent covers were fuzzy with rust, and it was obvious the wiring and plumbing would have to be completely redone. But the worst part was all the *stuff:* "When we first viewed the place, we were so overwhelmed by the owners' mess, we almost rejected the building on sight," said Meryl.

Lucia said, "They were the kind of pack rats who saved piles of newspapers from the past twenty years."

"But the most bizarre element was that there were little bowls everywhere," said Meryl. "We thought they were cat dishes, but the real estate agent explained—rather sheepishly, I might add—that each one contained a few ounces of holy water."

Lucia added, "And there were posters of Jesus in every room."

"Not that we don't approve of Christian themes—we're churchgoing Methodists ourselves. I would be very happy with a Fra Filippo Lippi over my mantle, but these were on the tacky side. And the fact that they were taped to the walls—it made you think the occupants were just a bit off their noodles."

Reminding themselves that they were buying the rooms, not the contents of the rooms, Lucia and Meryl took a more serious look at the place. One of their major negotiating points, however, was to insist that the sellers remove each and every personal item from the apartment. "We had nightmares about having to deal with eleven tons of newspapers," said Lucia.

When the Wisconsin sisters had their closing on the building, their real estate agent assured them that the other family, en route to a house in the suburbs, was busily packing up and shipping out the detritus of their life in Boston. On the day the new owners were set to take possession, they saw to their satisfaction that the first floor was empty and broom-swept. But as they climbed to their living quarters on the third floor, they were dismayed to see that though all the furniture, newspapers, and knick-knacks had been eliminated, the tired religious posters still clung to the walls, and the bowls of holy water lurked everywhere—on the mantle, on window sills, on kitchen counters, and in corners of rooms on the floor.

"Thank God we hadn't planned on actually living there for many months," said Meryl. They'd known in advance that renovations would be time-consuming, and accordingly the sisters had sublet a sunny, cheerful apartment two blocks closer to the river. "Still, we had no clue as to how to deal with the religious artifacts. We felt superstitious about tossing them all away." They salved their conscience by tipping the water into a ceramic pot of hydrangeas, bought expressly for the purpose. The posters they carefully stripped from the walls, stacked, rolled into a cardboard tube and deposited in a Red Cross bin near Kenmore Square. The multi-blessed hydrangea accompanied them to their riverfront apartment and there, on a sunny ledge behind the breakfast nook, it thrived, sending out globes of blue flowers into the dead of winter.

The following spring, the sisters moved into their new apartment. "It was totally unrecognizable from what it had been," recalled Meryl.

"Thank God!" said Lucia. "Our contractor had thoroughly gutted the place, sheetrocked, raised the ceiling, added sky-lights, and put in new windows, new floors, new everything. It was a dream apartment."

"Until we moved into it," added Meryl.

Their first evening, they ate dinner seated at their new maple-topped table from Crate & Barrel. Afterward, they set-tled down in the living room and Lucia decided to light a com-pressed sawdust log in the newly renovated brick fireplace.

"Our contractor had declared it cleaned, vetted, flu open, and ready for business," she said, thinking back to that night. Unfortunately, when she lit a match and touched it to the paper wrapping, an orange spark shot up, but the normally super-flammable material refused to ignite. She tried lighting a paper towel and chucking it under the log, but the flame fizzled out as quickly and completely as if an invisible hose had been trained on the fireplace. She shook her head and resolved to speak to the contractor in the morning.

Later, seated on wing chairs, the sisters faced each other across the cold hearth, and sipping Frangelica, discussed plans for the store downstairs. Suddenly, from the middle of the room, halfway between them and the bay windows overlooking the street, a low growl rose up from the floor. Both sisters jumped from their seats and said in unison, "What was that?"

They weren't able to determine the source of the noise, and all pleasure at relaxing in their living room drained away. They decided to make an early night of it, but as they moved toward the hallway, another growl, this time generated from under the living room lintel, froze them in place. Another growl from the original source revved behind them.

"It was as if we were trapped in our living room by an invisible circle of wolves," said Meryl.

They held hands and made a dash for the hallway, terrified that as they ran actual canine teeth might rip into their calves. Nothing of the sort happened, but they were badly shaken as they changed into pajamas and climbed into bed. "We each had our own bedroom," said Lucia, "but that night we shared the double bed in Meryl's room, and left the light on. We nervously joked that it felt like we were back in grade school."

The next day and evening passed uneventfully, and so, in fact, did the following month. Meryl and Lucia stopped holding their breath. This initial respite allayed the sisters' fears and gave them hope that the strange phenomenon that had afflicted their living room was fleeting. Later, they realized that this lull, whether it happened spontaneously or out of some sinister design, misled them into settling in more than was wise, making it harder to later extricate themselves. Cheerfully, they bought furniture, experimented with pleasing pastels on the walls, socialized with friends, and just generally made of the third floor quarters a beloved new home. The potted hydrangea was the only note of failure during that peaceful period. Nurtured with holy water, it had flourished in the riverfront apartment, but it began to wilt almost immediately in the new quarters. By the end of the month, it died.

And then the reign of terror began.

The growls returned to the living room almost nightly. The sisters took to shunning the room, but the entire apartment seemed to have turned against them. Lucia was seated at the kitchen table one morning when the overhead light fixture wrenched free of its mooring. Lucia bobbed away and the lamp missed her head by inches, landing on the table with a crash. Other electrical outlets began to administer small but vexing shocks. Both sisters slipped on puddles of greasy water that appeared for no discernible reason. During the night, they were frequently awakened by the sound of hurtling objects in the front rooms. In the morning, they'd find books dumped on the floor, paintings out of kilter, and chairs knocked over.

"The most confounding thing that ever happened," said Lucia, "was the time the front door wouldn't close. I examined it closely and saw that the thingamajig that sticks in and out to open and shut the door was in a stiff position and couldn't be budged. I compared it to other doors and discovered it was screwed on backward. I dug out my tool kit, disassembled the entire doorknob, and turned the thingamajig the right way, but what was that all about? No human agent would bother to switch that around. Not even a burglar would have any reason to do that. All he would be interested in doing was picking the lock, not jamming it up. Besides, there was nothing missing from the apartment."

The sisters delayed opening the bookstore downstairs until they got a handle on why the top floor of their building was beset by demons. They invited a psychic friend, Joan Flanders, to visit and see if she could detect any hidden sensations. Joan, a petite, pretty woman of Filipino descent, has an intuitive medical practice on the Cape. She sat in a rocking chair in the living room and closed her eyes. The sisters watched her intently as her exhalations lengthened and her body grew abnormally still. In a faraway voice she said, "There was a battered wife who lived here. It was a long time ago. She suffered so deeply, all the time. Finally, . . ." A look of anguish crossed Joan's face, "the husband bashed her head with a heavy kitchen thing . . . some kind of wooden mallet. She . . . she died. The husband shot himself. When their spirits left their bodies, he tried to keep her from going into the Light, but she called upon all the guardian angels who had ever taken pity on her to carry her away. I see a tornado of blinding white light. The husband closes his arms around emptiness. For a long, long time he haunted these rooms, afraid to proceed to the afterlife for fear of the retribution awaiting him there. He's gone now. Maybe somehow he was exorcized, persuaded to leave, but he left behind a vortex that's filled with negative energy. It's like the stink left behind when algae floats up from the bottom of a pond and putrefies on the surface."

Later, when Joan came out of her trance, the sisters asked what they should do to cleanse the apartment of the evil ghost's stale energies. They told her about the bowls of holy water and the Jesus posters left by prior owners. Joan nodded. "Those things may have helped."

The next order of business, the sisters decided, was to acquire their own holy water. But how would a couple of middle-aged Methodist ladies go about getting their hands on that? As far as they knew, the Catholic clergy was its sole purveyor.

They called upon Cousin Francine, who lived in Saugus, and who'd briefly been a nun. Five days later Francine showed up at their door with a plastic lemonade pitcher of holy water. Ever after, she made a bimonthly visit to the city bearing a fresh supply.

These days Lucia and Meryl laugh at the lengths to which they went to collect aesthetically pleasing receptacles for their holy water. "We had a favorite ceramic shop in Copley Square," said Meryl, "and we got some white Neuwirth bowls there. We went antiquing and found all sorts of delightful containers. My favorite was a silver mercury bowl—a very popular item in Victorian times."

They distributed vessels of holy water around each of the rooms, just as the prior occupants had done before them. Lucia said, "We also opened all the windows and doors and asked the spirits to leave—please."

In addition, they burned sage and lavender, as Joan had advised them to do.

And the results?

The apartment quieted down pretty much as it had in the first month of the sisters' tenancy. They opened the bookstore and tea room and for several years enjoyed modest success until they sold the building in 1992. Lucia explains, "We both have independent income to fall back on, so we decided to spend more time traveling and less time ringing up sales on the cash register."

The new owners sent the sisters a letter to inform them that occasionally articles go missing from their apartment, but they've learned to be patient—almost everything shows up again in time, and when it does it's right in the most obvious place where they'd already hunted for it. Meryl and Lucia made a full disclosure at the time of sale, and the new owners have decided that compared to the hauntings the sisters endured, a minor bit of poltergeist activity is nothing to get worked up about.

Looking back, Meryl and Lucia recall that even after the haunting abated, they never quite let down their guard. Neither sister would spend the night alone in their dwelling. If a situation arose that took one of them away from the city, the other made plans to decamp as well. "Once I was sitting home alone at eleven-thirty at night," said Lucia, "and Meryl called to tell me her flight had been delayed out of Atlanta, and she wouldn't be home till the next morning. I wasted no time. I called the Marriott on the Wharf and reserved a room. That apartment wasn't the kind of place you ever wanted to stay in without someone to say 'nighty-night' to."

PART II

Literary & Historic Ghosts

Parker House Hotel at corner of Beacon and Tremont Streets
Photo by E.E. Bond, 1900–1910. BOSTON PUBLIC LIBRARY PRINTS DEPT.

Some of our most revered
authors of ghost stories have either originated
in Boston or spent abundant time in the city,
among them: Edgar Allan Poe,
Nathaniel Hawthorne, Edith Wharton,
Henry James, and H.P. Lovecraft.
Why is that? What exactly was it about Boston
that steered them to write, at some point
in their careers, about the supernatural?
Read on, and maybe you'll begin to understand
how the fabric of Boston's history
was woven so sweetly and inextricably
with the macabre.

⊨ 5 ⊫

The Real Cask of Amontillado

If you know the background of Edgar Allan Poe's short story *The Cask of Amontillado*, you can better appreciate the significance of the Roving Skeleton of Boston Bay. Poe, the father of classic horror literature, was born in Boston on January 19, 1809. *Amontillado*, arguably his finest short story, is a lurid and brilliant tale of a man bricked up alive in a dungeon. It's based on a true story that Poe uncovered with the persistence and cunning of a modern-day investigative reporter.

In 1827, when Poe was a young lad of eighteen, he enlisted in the Army, and his first posting placed him at Fort Independence on Castle Island in Boston Harbor. The first stirrings of his literary muse led him to explore his new army post in ways that definitely did not follow military form. A small monument outside the walls caught his attention, and one Sunday he set out early and wandered to the water's edge to get a closer look. On the western side of the stout obelisk he read the following lines: "The officers of the U.S. Regiment of Lt. Art'y erected this monument as a testimony of their respect and friendship for an amiable man & gallant officer."

Thoughtfully, Poe circled to the eastern panel and came across this fragment from an ode by poet William Collins:

"Here honour comes, a Pilgrim gray / To deck the turf that wraps his clay."

Poe sat and brooded for a while, and then he rounded the monument to face the northern side, facing Boston, where he read: "Beneath this stone are deposited the remains of Lieutenant ROBERT F. MASSIE, of the U.S. Regt. of Light Artillery. Near this spot on the 25th Dec 1817, fell Lieutenant Robert F. Massie, Aged 21 years."

Poe copied the inscriptions in his notebook. He felt a rising excitement at the drama captured in the terse wording of the monument. He could almost hear the clang of swords in the biting sea air of ten years previous. A duel had been fought on this spot, he realized, and for some reason the military brass had determined to keep the details a secret. That was all that the budding author needed to track down the story. He began to ask a host of questions of anyone who would open up to him. Thanks to his detective ability, he assembled a complete picture.

In the summer of 1817, an affable young lieutenant named Robert F. Massie arrived at the fort to take up his duties. A popular fellow, he nonetheless invited the enmity and jealousy of the one officer who was too antisocial to respond to his charm and goodwill. Captain Green had already developed a reputation for being a bully who backed up his maliciousness with expert swordsmanship. Every last man in the regiment tried steered clear of him, but it was impossible to avoid him entirely on that tiny army post surrounded by water.

On Christmas Eve, Massie and Green and a handful of other officers sat down to a winter's evening of cards. With snow sticking to the windows and wind howling under the eaves, the stakes of the game intensified. Around midnight Lieutenant Massie threw down a winning hand and scooped up the pile of coins in the center of the table.

Captain Green leaped up and struck Massie across the face. "You're a cheat!" he hollered. "I demand immediate satisfaction!"

The blood drained from the young Virginian's face, but the protocol for these matters was implacable; he was forced to accept the challenge.

The men and their seconds met at daybreak outside the walls of the fort. Christmas morning broke clear but stingingly cold. Bells clanged from nearby buoys and gulls squawked overhead. In time-honored tradition, the seconds pleaded with the duelists to forgive and forget. Also as tradition dictated, the men declined to reconcile. As Poe would imagine the scene ten years later, swords clanged in the air. But Green had the advantage; not only was he the more skillful swordsman, he was also a stone-cold killer, a sociopath, and within seconds he drove his blade through Massie's rib cage. The lieutenant crumpled to the sand, clutching his wound. His men carried him to the infirmary, where he died that afternoon.

The officers of Fort Independence suffered from acute depression in the weeks succeeding their comrade's death. Conversations were muted, and men shuffled mechanically through their appointed rounds, expressions mournful. Some action had to be taken to vent their frustration and craving for justice.

Two events occurred nearly simultaneously: A monument was erected to Massie on the very spot where he'd been run through by Green's sword, and the bully of Castle Island disappeared. He was never seen or heard from again, and after an appropriate amount of time, Captain Green was entered into the books as a deserter.

But the inquisitive Edgar Allan Poe probed deeper and discovered what had really become of the evil swordsman. After the fateful duel, Massie's friends learned that at other

military outposts Green had previously badgered six other
officers into lethal combat. He had, in other words, found a
legally sanctioned method for committing serial murders.

One night a delegation of officers visited Green in his
chamber, and faking friendliness, plied him with spirits. When
the big bully became roaring drunk, they treated him to still
more alcohol until he'd reached the falling down stage. Two of
the heftiest soldiers clung to either side of him, and with the
other officers in tow, lugged the drunken brute down to one
of the many old dungeons. An earlier search had yielded the
most remote and disused of the dingy cells. They dragged
the limp captain through the narrow opening and stretched
him out on the floor, shackling him to iron handcuffs and
footcuffs that had long ago manacled the extremities of other
wretched prisoners.

Midway through the operation, Captain Green came out
of his stupor and demanded to know what was going on. The
men ignored his shouts and trudged out into the passageway,
where earlier they'd deposited the materials they would need
to complete their dark task. As Green went on hoarsely shouting for release, the men mixed mortar with water and piled
layer of brick on layer of brick. Presently, the drunken captain's shouts were silenced, encapsulated by thick walls.

It must have taken several days for Captain Green to die
an agonizing death.

To evade detection, the men who'd shanghaied their
officer filed for transfers to other outposts, but before they
shipped out, words of their covert action were whispered to
some of the enlisted men. It wasn't difficult, then, for Poe to
track down the truth about the captain's terrible fate.

But it wasn't a story that the higher-ranking officers
wanted exposed. Before Poe could fire another question or
scribble another note, he was summoned to the desk of the
post commander, where the following dialogue took place:

POST COMMANDER: I understand that you've been asking questions about Massie's monument and the duel which he fought?

EDGAR ALLAN POE: I have, sir.

COMMANDER: And I understand that you've learned all about the subsequent events connected with the duel?

POE: I have, sir.

COMMANDER: Well, you are never to tell that story outside the walls of the fort.

Poe, when he agreed, allowed *tell* to serve as the operative word. We can almost imagine him crossing his fingers behind his back as he reasoned that *tell* was a thing apart from *write*. Many years later he sat down to compose *The Cask of Amontillado*. Although the tale is set in Europe, with fictional characters, it's still easy to distinguish the nuts and bolts—or iron and bricks—of the incident at Fort Independence.

Nearly a century after the duel, in 1905, a work crew dispatched to Castle Island came upon the oldest basement of the fort. The workmen saw that in one dank section, the pattern of cells departed from the original plan. In other words, they were missing a dungeon. One of the engineers ran his torchlight over the wall and found a small bricked-up area. Additional lanterns and pickaxes were delivered to the site, and after a couple of hours a hole was opened up in the wall. The smallest man in the group shimmied inside with a lantern. Almost immediately, he launched himself out again, in his haste leaving his lamp behind.

"There's a skeleton in there."

After a few more hours of hacking down the wall, the crew assembled around the ghastly sight of a skeleton, wrists and ankles encircled by decaying manacles. A few threads of an 1812 army uniform clung to the bones. Lacking modern-day forensics, the remains could not be identified. The skeleton was interred like any other army officer, with a military funeral and burial in the cemetery on Castle Island. His grave is marked "unknown."

The remains of Lieutenant Massie, on the other hand, were moved around more than the young man had ever traveled in life. His monument attracted thousands of visitors to the fort on weekends, particularly after a bridge connected the island to Boston proper in 1891. The next year, the monument and Massie's remains were removed to Governor's Island and the new cemetery at that location. In 1908 Massie was again disinterred and carted, along with his famous monument, across the water to Deer Island to find sanctuary in the Resthaven Cemetery. Finally (one hopes), in 1939, Massie and his tombstone were moved halfway across the state to Fort Devens in Ayer, Massachusetts.

No one knows why it was deemed necessary to keep the body in constant rotation, but due to the fact that Robert F. Massie's remains were buried four times in different locales within 122 years, the lieutenant's relics became known as the Roving Skeleton of Boston Bay.

There are those who've visited Fort Independence who claim that a more ethereal part of the long-dead Virginian remains forever on the shores of the little outpost at the southeastern edge of the city.

⊹= 6 =⊹

Fort Warren's Lady in Black

If you think Scarlet O'Hara and Rhett Butler were the only passionate lovers of the Civil War era, think again. (And Scarlet and Rhett weren't even real.) In 1861, when a young Southern soldier named Andrew Lanier was summoned to battle, he begged for—and received—a short leave to go and propose to his intended. Without a moment to spare, he hurled himself on his horse and galloped to Crawfordville, Georgia. Dusty and bedraggled, he arrived at his lady love's home, fell on bended knee, and asked her to marry him. She said yes, and the ceremony took place on June 28, 1861. They had forty-eight hours of honeymoon bliss before young Lanier saddled up his horse for his journey back to his company. His bride wept, as so many brides, North and South, were weeping at that very moment. The young groom tried to rally her spirits as well as his own by whistling their favorite song, "Drink to Me Only with Thine Eyes." Before long, she whistled along with him, though tears continued to spill down her cheeks.

At the end of the summer, Andrew Lanier was knocked unconscious in battle and subsequently taken prisoner. Along with scores of other Southern captives, he was shipped to

Fort Warren, colloquially known as the Corridor of Dungeons, on George's Island in Boston Harbor.

Back in Crawfordville, his bride received a letter from her husband imparting news of his capture, of the frightful conditions at the prison, of how lonely he felt, and of how much he missed her. He wrote that he despaired of ever seeing her again, for it seemed perfectly clear that with disease and starvation vanquishing prisoners to the right and left of him, he would surely die in this dreadful place. In spite of this anticipated ignominious end, however, his life had been worth living for the short duration that he'd loved and been loved by her.

Those proved to be fighting words for Mrs. Lanier. As she clutched the letter to her breast, she put forward a desperate plan—her own small, savage Civil War to save her beloved. Telling no one of her scheme, she stole into town and obtained a suit of men's clothes, a pepperbox pistol, and a pipeline to a trusty blockade runner. She cut her hair, donned shirt and trousers, and boarded the blockade runner's vessel. Days later, the seaman put her ashore on a dark windy stretch of Cape Cod. Disguised as a young Yankee male, Mrs. Lanier journeyed to Hull, Massachusetts, where she sought shelter with a Southern sympathizer. None of the neighbors could possibly guess that the young soft-spoken traveling lad was a desolate bride hellbent on freeing her man.

For days on end, Mrs. Lanier stood on the beach and trained a telescope on the George's Island fort, less than a mile from shore. She soon knew intimately the guard booths, barracks, parade ground, and grim stone walls of the Corridor of Dungeons.

On the first stormy night, January 15, 1862, she made her move. A pelting rain produced funnels of gray mist backlit by lightning and rocked by thunder. In the midst of this gothic weather, Mrs. Lanier's host rowed her across the channel to

George's Island and deposited her on the beach. He tossed her a woolen bundle containing her pepperbox pistol and a short-handed pickax, then he waved farewell as thunder and lightning cracked around the tiny vessel.

The lady saboteur crouched behind a sea wall. She watched as two sentries, their black cloaks soaked through, slowly walked toward each other, nodded, then turned and strode some fifty paces in opposite directions. Earlier, by telescope, Mrs. Lanier had timed the protocol: she had ninety seconds to scurry between the guards before they returned.

She sprinted through the battering rain and dove into a tangle of bushes. Gasping for breath, she peered out to watch the sentries meet, turn, and once again head off in opposite directions. She shot to her feet, tucked her bundle under her jacket, and shinnied up the jagged stone wall of the prison. Over the top she somersaulted, landing with a thump in the muddy courtyard. She remained prone in a puddle, glancing to the right and left of her for passing sentries. No one seemed to be anywhere nearby. Within and without, the Corridor of Dungeons slept under the steady barrage of rain. Mrs. Lanier rose stiffly and moved stealthily toward the nearest aperture of barred window. Hope, excitement, and fear thudded in her chest as she whistled "Drink to Me Only with Thine Eyes."

No one answered.

She tried again, waiting in the foul night as rain poured over her. Had the prison been evacuated? Was her husband still here? Her heart pounded as she realized how foolish she'd been to count on his continuing presence at Fort Warren. Nearly three months had elapsed since she'd received his letter. Anything could have happened—he could be languishing in some other Yankee hell-hole hundreds of miles from here. He could be dead. Fighting defeat, she threw back her shoulders and let loose with a long, shrill, frantic whistle. The silence persisted, rain drumming down. Then an answering whistle sailed out through the high slit in the walls. In another minute a twisted bed sheet descended. Mrs. Lanier grabbed hold and hoisted herself up the slimy, wet wall. Many hands reached out to pull her petite, sopping wet frame through the narrow opening. She found herself in black depths lit by dingy kerosene lanterns. She smelled the stench of old walls and overpowering mildew, and the next thing she knew her husband's arms were wrapped around her.

Andrew Lanier and his comrades whisked their visitor into a central dungeon where a secret committee had been meeting and plotting escape for all six hundred Confederate soldiers. Earlier, they had planned to dig a tunnel under the fort to the shore where a schooner would be waiting for them, courtesy of Southern sympathizers. But now with the arrival of the lady from Georgia, and she in possession of a short-handed pickax, another more daring procedure presented itself: they would dig inward, rather than out, coming up under the parade grounds. From that vantage point they would break into the arsenal, arm themselves, and quickly immobilize the eighty Union soldiers guarding the prison. From that point, the tide of war would turn to the Rebel cause as they trained all 248 cannons of Fort Warren against the city of Boston.

For many weeks, work on the tunnel progressed. The soldiers devised an elaborate system of chores and subterfuges. Each day, they began before the morning checkup, with a pile of earth massing at the front of the tunnel. When the guards strolled by, a group of prisoners would lounge on the mound to hide it. At the lengthening end of the tunnel, a rotating crew of men hacked away underground while other crews loaded the earth into hammocks made of their shirts and bore it out to the far window slits where they cast it to the winds. A handful of men with engineering skills plotted and re-plotted the direction of the tunnel, sometimes canceling out days and nights of work by changing the angle of the dig.

At last the team with the pickax stood ready to take its final jabs at the earth that lay between the granite stones of the fort and the center of the parade ground. It was one o'clock in the morning when an exultant lieutenant hefted the tool overhead, then heaved it toward the top of the tunnel, slicing through the earth and crashing hard on the stone wall of the bastion.

Nearby, a sentry heard the sharp sound of metal striking rock.

The sentry sounded the alarm. Shouts erupted from the guard booth. Doors clanged open and shut. The sergeant on duty alerted the commander of Fort Warren, an artillery expert named Justin Dimmock, of Marblehead. Colonel Dimmock and a platoon of men charged the Corridor of Dungeons. At the far end, they saw a group of ragged men heaving clods of earth through window slits.

Under a starless sky, the Southerners were rounded up in the courtyard. The sergeant took roll call. He was short eleven prisoners. Colonel Dimmock inspected every inch of the walls until he found the opening to the tunnel. He shouted down the shaft for the holdouts to surrender. In abject defeat, ten men straggled out. Still inside the shaft, the Laniers hatched one last desperate scheme.

Colonel Dimmock shouted into the opening that he still lacked one prisoner. Slowly, sheepishly, Andrew Lanier crept out with his hands over his head. A phalanx of guards surrounded him. The Union soldiers crowed at the successful capture of every last Southerner. And just as the men in blue began to breathe easy, Mrs. Lanier leapt from the mouth of the tunnel and plugged the snout of her pepperbox pistol to the neck of the nearest guard. She cocked the gun and demanded the surrender of Colonel Dimmock and his eighty-man guard unit.

The colonel raised his hands and slowly advanced toward the hostage taker. He spoke soothingly to her, gentleman to young lady, transporting her back to her belle-of-the-ball days, when she wore crinolines and satin slippers and she never in a thousand years would have imagined herself thrusting pistols into the necks of Union soldiers. Colonel Dimmock promised the Confederate bride full cooperation. She let out a long sigh just before the commander lunged forward to knock her weapon from her grasp. The rusty old pistol exploded, firing a metal fragment into the brain of her young husband.

A lonely cemetery sat at the fringes of the fort. Two days after the failed escape attempt, Andrew Lanier was buried without ceremony or marker. Colonel Dimmock declared the widow a spy and ordered her execution for February 2, 1862.

An hour before she was set to hang, the woman's guards asked if she had a last request. As a matter of fact, she had: "I'm tired of wearing this man's suit of clothes. I'd like to put on a gown once more before I die." Needless to say, the fort had a dearth of women's outfits. After searching high and low, the guards uncovered a theatrical trunk left behind by the First Corps of Cadets from a previous summer tour. A black robe such as something an actress might have donned in a production of *Medea* was delivered to the doomed prisoner. Mrs. Lanier pulled the robe over her slender shoulders, and minutes later, the noose descended over her head.

In the afternoon, the soldiers cut her body down and interred it beside that of her husband in the forlorn little cemetery.

Some weeks later, a private named Richard Cassidy pulled the dubious night duty of patrolling the area where Mrs. Lanier's gallows had stood. With a fog moving in from the ocean, he realized he was none too happy about finding himself alone at this spot, so fraught with sorrowful memories. All of a sudden, he felt a pair of hands slip around his throat and squeeze hard. He wrenched around to confront his attacker. He found his face only inches from Mrs. Lanier's, her features contorted with rage. Clad in the flowing black robe, she looked exactly as she'd done on the day she'd been hanged. Her grip on his jugular felt as real—and as lethal—as a choking dealt by a living assassin. Cassidy summoned a terrified burst of strength and shoved her away. He fled to the guardhouse, screaming all the way.

The other soldiers laughed at his story, but the humor was lost on Private Cassidy, who refused to return to his post the following night and was forced to pay for his insubordination with thirty days in lock-up.

Since that night, the Lady in Black, as Mrs. Lanier's apparition has come to be known, has been observed by a variety of Fort Warren residents and visitors. In the winter of 1891, four officers out for a stroll on the leeward side of the island came upon an odd set of footprints in the snow, unmistakably formed by a lady's slippers. Not a single woman lived at the fort, nor for that matter, had any women even visited in the past many months, unless unbeknownst to them, another desperate bride had smuggled herself ashore in the night. The officers attributed the footprints to the Lady in Black. By that time, it was taken as an article of faith that from time to time the Georgia bride's hatred for the North conjured her back from the grave.

And she kept on coming. During World War II, a sentry posted at the site of the gallows collapsed in screaming fits. The doctor on the base shipped him to a psychiatric facility where he remained for several decades. A few years after the sentry lost his mind, Captain Charles I. Norris, of Towson, Maryland, was alone one night in the library of his home. As he read, he felt a tap on his shoulder. He turned to find no one in the room with him. With a shrug, he returned to his book and once again an invisible hand touched his shoulder. The upstairs phone rang, and Captain Norris set his book aside to climb the stairs to answer, but the phone stopped ringing before he reached it. He dialed the base operator and asked, "Who was it that just called me, Operator?"

"Your wife answered on your end, sir, and took the message."

"My wife? My wife is not on the island."

Captain Norris returned to his library and sank into his chair, shaking his head. Between the taps on his shoulder and the mysterious woman answering the phone in his own house, he accepted with a groan of incredulity that the infamous Lady in Black had paid him a call. It was bound to happen sooner or later.

Since that time, thousands of visitors have thronged the old historic fort, and the ghostly legend is part of what draws them. Guests to Fort Warren stand little chance, however, of observing anything of an occult nature. There is little likelihood of mobs of tourists flushing from hiding a spirit as elusive as Mrs. Lanier's. And, conceivably, the Rebel bride has given up on making her occasional forays, which seemed to be motivated by a vengefulness that survived her execution and spanned many decades. In short, the Civil War is long over, and it's comforting to think that, given time in the afterlife, our more fiery passions can be neutralized.

Mr. and Mrs. Lanier's remains were long ago transferred to unknown resting places, but their hearts that beat as one may still hover over Fort Warren—love being the single human emotion that does, in fact, endure.

⇌ 7 ⇌

Peter Rugg Rides Again

This is one of those ghost stories that is just far enough over the top—like Anne Boleyn walking the Tower of London "with 'er head tucked underneath 'er arm"—to make us wonder how much of it is true. Suffice it to say that people who've encountered this legendary apparition were ready to swear in court that they saw what they saw.

Before the American Revolution, cattle dealer Peter Rugg lived a comfortable middle-class life in a middle-class house on Middle Street in Boston. He had a devoted wife and an adorable young daughter, and his neighbors could rely on him to pay his assessments and volunteer for the fire brigade. His one notable flaw was a hair-trigger temper. Any little irritation or injustice, real or imagined, could set him off. Those who were close to him worried that sooner or later his fury would land him in real trouble.

One sunny fall day, Peter Rugg hitched up his enormous Roman-nosed bay horse to a contrastingly small carriage, and with his daughter along for the ride, set off to Concord to conduct some business with a colleague in the livestock trade. On the return trip, late in the afternoon, father and daughter stopped at a favorite tavern in West Cambridge (then known as Menotomy), Miss Rugg for a cup of cocoa, Mr. Rugg for a hot spiced rum to lend cheer to the last leg of the journey. Their host, Tom Cutter, pulled up a chair at their table by the fire, and imbibed a number of spiced rums of his own. Looking beyond Peter Rugg, the tavern keeper saw through the mullioned window that the sky was "smurrin' up" to the south, with lightning sizzling in the underbelly of the black clouds.

"You best be staying here for the night, Rugg, my man. Looks like we're in for a right witch's brew of a storm."

Rugg glanced out the window but appeared unfazed. He rose and placed a coin on the table. "It's nothin' 'twill keep me from my own bed."

As the Ruggs started out the door, Tom Cutter charged after them. "Don't be a fool, Rugg! Night will soon be here, and this pelting rain will be the death of your daughter. Can you not see the storm increases in violence?"

"Let the storm increase. I will see home tonight in spite of storm or the Devil, or may I never see home!"

Perhaps Tom Cutter was too woozy from spiced rum, or else he failed to recognize his customer's signs of mounting ire—the growl in Rugg's throat, the intent, staring eyes—but as the cattle dealer bundled his girl onto the rig, the tavern keeper grabbed the man's arm to detain him. Furious, Peter Rugg tossed off the hand with a shrug that landed a punch on Tom Cutter's nose. The tavern keeper staggered back at the same time that Peter Rugg's whip lashed the back of his horse. A jag of lightning rent the sky and thunder exploded. The steed reared up with a shriek and galloped off into the teeth of the storm. Tom Cutter fell back against the lintel of his doorway, aghast as he saw the small carriage swallowed up by charcoal-colored flumes of rain.

Peter Rugg and his daughter never returned alive to their home on Middle Street.

Mrs. Rugg rallied her neighbors and the constabulary to

search for her husband and child. As the weeks went by, and snow covered the narrow streets of Colonial Boston, the poor woman fell grief-stricken into the slow, dark months of the first winter of her bereavement.

And then, after the winds of March and balmy breezes of April had dried up the cobblestones, Peter Rugg raced his carriage down Middle Street again.

It was a drizzling night in May, long past midnight, when Thomas Felt, a gunsmith, bolted awake at the clatter of a horse's hooves. In those quiet times, when people crawled into bed after sundown and arose before the rooster crowed, it could only mean trouble when a carriage tore across the stones at this late hour. The gunsmith lurched to the window. He gazed at the narrow lane that ran between rows of dormered wood-and-stone walls. From the west end of the lane a conveyance came rattling over the uneven cobbles. The rig flew past his window, and the gunsmith caught a glimpse of Peter Rugg and his daughter. Rugg's huge Roman-nosed bay whinnied loudly. A glow of blue phosphorescence surrounded the carriage, trailing sparks behind it. As the spectral horse and passengers scrambled by, a surge of frigid air swirled up to his dormer window, enveloping the gunsmith and causing his teeth to chatter.

Over the years, news of Rugg sightings circulated throughout Boston. At the Charlestown Bridge, the toll taker swore that on several occasions he'd spotted the cattle dealer lathering his horse along the quay, his daughter clinging to his arm. Each time, Rugg blazed past the toll taker without stopping to pay his fee. On one occasion, the tender, infuriated by this uncivil treatment, jumped off his stool and hurled it at the passing steed. The stool passed straight through the monstrous dark horse and bounced off the farthest guardrail.

Another time, in another part of town, the stagecoach from Providence nearly collided with a carriage clipping up from the crossroads. The driver of the private rig tugged at the reins and called up to the stage to ask the route to Boston. A passenger inside the coach, a sea captain from Rhode Island, observed a man and a little girl, both of them soaking wet—a surprising sight as the skies blazed with sunshine. The stagecoach driver waved the man and child ahead of him, and the little rig disappeared in a dust cloud of motion. A few minutes later, traveling from the same southwesterly road that had yielded up the rig, a sudden thunder shower passed over the stagecoach, deluging the driver and horses and splashing the passengers through the open windows.

Throughout the next century and a half, reports of Rugg encounters cropped up from time to time throughout New England. At one point a Boston journalist interviewed a peddler who had this to say about the phantom rig driver: "I was unfortunate enough to see the man and his carriage within a fortnight, in four different states, and each time I was shortly afterward visited by heavy thunderstorms. If I meet them once more, I shall be forced to take out marine insurance on my wares."

In the 1860s, a stage coachdriver, one Adonariah Adams of the Portland Mail, a normally genial man, gave the following doleful account: "One day after we drove through Newburyport, I noticed thunderheads in the southern sky and whipped the horses into a trot. Ahead of us, heavy streaks of lightning flashed across the horizon, and I realized that we were in for a nasty tempest. We ascended Witch-Hang Hill at a fast clip, and as we reached the top, something compelled me to look back. There I saw Peter Rugg's carriage tearing after us and gaining fast. My horses took fright and began to run at a desperate and dangerous pace, but Rugg's great beast steadily gained until he was racing neck-and-neck with my wheel horses. Suddenly, a bolt of lightning struck the Rugg conveyance. In the instantaneous flash, I saw Peter and his daughter glowing with fire like a horseshoe as it is taken from a black-smith's hearth. At the same time, flames and sparks cascaded from the mouth and ears of the huge bay horse and I was al-most stiffed by the odor of brimstone, yet the bolt seemed to have no effect on the creature, for the carriage continued on. My horses were so frightened that they leaped from the road, wrecking the coach against the boulder. It is my opinion that what I saw was the Devil's shade of Peter Rugg."

The last Rugg incident occurred in the early 1900s, when an itinerant preacher named Samuel Nickles made his way on horseback from Wickford, Rhode Island, to Providence. He'd tucked his sparse belongings in his saddlebag, but he carried his Bible in his left hand, either for inspiration or in case he might need it for an impromptu sermon along the way. As he and his horse, Romeo, neared Quonset, they were caught in a violent thunderstorm. The Reverend Nickles hunched his shoulders against the rain while Romeo plodded between two hills that narrowed the road to a single lane. Suddenly, from the opposite direction, came the clatter of a horse. Samuel Nickles stared in fright at a giant bay dragging a small carriage and charging hell-for-leather in his direction. The bay's eyes glowed reddish gold. On the seat of the rig a man and a small girl huddled together against an annihilating rain.

A crash was imminent in the narrow pass. Romeo reared up, spun halfway around, and flung his rider at the galloping bay. The Reverend Nickles landed smack across the back of the oncoming steed. He grabbed the beast's neck, shouting, "Stop! Stop!"

Lightning seared the sky, and a cannon blast of thunder rocked the ground, fracturing the air around them. The bay shrieked and leapt up, knocking the preacher to the earth, where he lay unconscious for several hours. When the poor man finally opened his eyes, he saw the sun shining in a cloud-less sky and Romeo grazing in a nearby plot of grass. Nickles rose stiffly to his feet to behold a pair of cloven hoof marks emblazoned in the bedrock.

The preacher made his circuit of camp meetings, telling and retelling the story of the steed of Satan and his lost passengers churning through their own personal maelstrom. Pilgrims and tourists alike trekked to Quonset to see the hoof marks in Devil's Foot Rock near Route One, an object of curiosity to this day. The Reverend Nickles's collision with the phantom rig was the last eyewitness account of a Peter Rugg apparition. Perhaps over the course of nearly one hundred fifty years, it took an honest preacher with a Bible in Peter Rugg's fateful ride home on a dark and stormy night.

⇒ 8 ⇐

The Ghost of Edith Wharton

The irony of it is sheerly stunning. As a child, the future famous author Edith Wharton was so terrified of the very idea of ghosts that, if she knew a book about the subject lurked in her father's study, she searched for the offending object and disposed of it immediately. She simply could not bear to lie in bed at night imagining a ghost book festering under the same roof with her. When we consider so phobic a child, it's almost impossible to accept that the girl could blossom into a woman who wrote ghost stories, among other things, and that she, herself, would become a ghost of some repute.

But first things first (and shortly we'll uncover Boston's claim on Ms. Wharton): In 1862, Edith was born into the wealthy New York Jones family. The expression "keeping up with the Joneses" is believed to refer to *those* Joneses. Edith showed no excessive fears for her first eight years, but everything changed in the summer of 1870, when the family was on holiday in the Black Forest of Germany. Edith had a near-fatal attack of typhoid fever. For several days she lay close to death, but at last the fever broke and she began weeks of slow recovery. During her time of convalescence, many well-wishers heaped her bed table with reading material, not all of it restful. One of the books, which for years she could only partially describe with a shudder as a "robber story," awakened her to a nether world of dark horrors, nameless dread, and the inescapable force field of the supernatural. It's hard to say why this single book should have been so damaging to her psyche. Perhaps in the depth of her illness she'd suffered hallucinations that had seemed all too real. The robber story frightened her so much that it led to a setback in her recovery, and until she reached her late twenties, when she seemed to snap out of it, she harbored a vague sense of jeopardy that rarely left her consciousness.

She also lived in fear of old houses. One of Edith's aunts resided alone in a gloomy twenty-four room mansion in Rhinecliff, New Jersey. Built in the Gothic style, it had dark shingles, hooded turrets, and probably a gargoyle or two peering down from a black granite cornice to scare the wits out of visiting nieces. Edith's occasional trips to the scary home, with its cribbed corridors and shutters banging in the wind, never failed to produce nightmares in the impressionable girl, nightmares that would persist for weeks after her visits.

Later in life Edith characterized herself as a "ghost-feeler." Whereas some people with psychic sensitivities can actually *see* spectral figures, Edith could enter a room and sense the presence of dead people as definitively as our nerve endings register heat or cold or our nostrils can pick up the stench of skunk or scent of cloves. In young adulthood she faced her fears and began reading the works of such horror-mongers as Edgar Allan Poe, Robert Lewis Stevenson, Joseph Sheridan Le Fanu, and many others. At last, the working out of her terror transmuted into her own art as she produced some of the finest ghost stories in the canon, among them "Bewitched," about a frantic wife in the backwoods of New England who turns to several pillars of the community to free her husband from the spell of a young lady, who happens to be dead;

"The Duchess at Prayer," also about adultery assisted by various spooky influences; and "The Looking Glass," about dark visions teleported through a mirror. Wharton's tales of mystery and terror engross the reader with their rich atmosphere and inscrutable characters, while the low-key pacing is fraught with fears of what might leap out from the shadows. As one English critic wrote after Wharton's death, "Her stories have a half-eerie, half-cozy charm of their own. You begin to feel the silence around your chair."

So, was all of this a dress rehearsal for Edith Wharton's subsequent appearance as a ghost? She'd lived in New York and Paris and visited often in Boston, where her dear friend and mentor, Henry James, had a townhouse at 131 Mount Vernon Street in Beacon Hill. The two famous authors could often be seen strolling arm-in-arm past the marble stairs and lofty bay windows of fashionable neighborhoods, any one of which could have served as a backdrop for either author's novels.

Oddly, all the important attachments of Wharton's life hailed from Boston, pulling her into and out of the city on every sojourn in America: The architect Ogden Codman, with whom she coauthored her first major work, *The Decoration of Houses*; Teddy Wharton, her long-suffering future ex-husband, who brought to the marriage a host of Boston in-laws; Sally Norton, her lifelong correspondent and closest female friend, daughter of the Harvard educator Charles Elliot Norton; Daniel Berkeley Updike, friend and mentor, and head of the Merrymount Press in Boston; W. Morton Fullerton, a journalist and object of Edith's romantic affections; Isabella Stuart Gardner, "Mrs. Jack," whose art collection at Fenway Court formed a focal point for Wharton's visits to the Massachusetts capital; and Henry James's brilliant siblings, William and Alice, Boston bonuses for anyone with an entree to that fabulous family.

Edith Wharton spent her entire adult life escaping the States, making a career out of the expatriate lifestyle in France, Italy, and England, and yet ... a mysterious tug from Massachusetts reeled her in, time and again (both alive, and, as we'll see, posthumously). Her fascination with this part of the American scene resulting in many fine short stories and three important novels: *Ethan Frome, Summer,* and *Fruit of the Tree.*

Wharton's love for New England found expression in her choice of a sprawling country home in Lenox, in the Berkshire Hills of western Massachusetts, the new stomping ground for Boston Brahmins and other assorted Yankee upper-crustniks of the eastern seaboard. In 1937, Edith died in Paris and was buried at Versailles, but it was to Lenox that her spirit winged its way.

Between 1900 and 1902, Edith and her husband, Teddy, had built The Mount, set on one hundred hilly acres. The size of a large hotel, the neo-Georgian mansion was the site of glittery summer salons when artists, writers, and socialites arrived for country weekends. In 1912 Wharton sold the house to Foxhollow Girls' School. After her death in 1937, stories abounded about ghostly visitations of the author in a high-collared white lace blouse, hair swept up in an Edwardian chignon, as she wandered through the upstairs rooms.

The stories have persisted ever since. In the 1980s, a theatre troupe called Shakespeare and Company bought The Mount and prepared to move in lock, stock, and costume trunk. The first person to enter the boarded-up mansion was a former priest turned actor and director named Dennis Karusnick. As he set about measuring the rooms, he heard footsteps dogging his own, yet a thorough search confirmed there was no one in the house with him that day. An actress named Tina Packer, after living at the Mount for several years, reported that she woke up one stormy night to see a man standing in her room with a somber expression on his face and his hair pulled back in a ponytail. She realized he was a ghost and, terrified, reverted to the time-honored dodge of pulling the covers over her head. After a few minutes she recovered her nerve and decided to take another peek. The ponytailed figure had disappeared.

Another actress named Andrea Haring told of her experience the night she decided to bed down on a mattress in the otherwise bare chamber of what had been Edith Wharton's study. Around four in the morning, she woke up because the fire had gone out and the room had turned frigid. When she opened her eyes, she saw three figures surrounded by opulent furnishings. Haring had been reading Wharton's biography, so she immediately recognized the famous lady author sprawled on a divan. Seated at a desk was a man with muttonchop whiskers who looked a lot like the secretary with whom Wharton was rumored to have had an affair. A third figure studied the other two with his arms folded across his chest. Haring realized he was the charming but somewhat obtuse Teddy, whom Edith had eventually divorced.

Haring reported, "I thought to myself, I wonder if I can leave? The minute the thought crossed my mind, all three of them looked at me." Edith gave her a dignified nod, and Teddy an aloof dismissal, but the man with the muttonchop whiskers beamed at her and bobbed his head in the affirmative. "I felt absolutely free to go at that point, which I did."

The spirits at The Mount weren't always so obliging. In the former servants' rooms on the top floor, now converted to dorms and offices, a hooded, cloaked figure has tried from time to time to restrain people forcibly from leaving their beds. After a frightening tussle, the spectral assailant dissolves into thin air. Other unexplained occurrences include the sound of fifteen or twenty children romping in empty gardens, a mysterious typing coming from the basement, and the sight of Edith, again dressed in one of her signature high-collared blouses, pacing the terrace.

By all accounts, The Mount is still haunted to this day. Perhaps Edith Wharton led such a charmed life, with her inestimable talent, double Pulitzer Prizes, her apartment in Paris, and her mansion in Lenox, that she's reluctant to give it up for her next incarnation. Wouldn't you be?

PART III

Boston's Ghostly Phenomena

Lightning over Back Bay and the Charles River, from Cambridge
Photo by E. E. Bond, c. 1910. BOSTON PUBLIC LIBRARY PRINTS DEPT.

Boston has harbored

more than its share of odd happenings.
As early as March 1639, the governor of the
Massachusetts Bay Colony, John Winthrop, wrote in
his journal about a luminous sphere flitting
over the northwestern horizon of town.
Other eyewitnesses observed the object darting
this way and that, its movements like those
of a pig zigging "hither and yon" to escape capture.
Later, in 1695, two similarly gleaming objects
chased each other across the dark skies of
Boston Harbor. Several spectators heard
a sepulchral voice through the clouds intoning,
"Boy, boy, come away, come away..."
Two weeks later, the play of lights returned,
and the mysterious summons was repeated.
In the following section, we'll take a look
at a few examples from Boston's bazaar
of the bizarre. ⇥

⇥ 9 ⇤

Boston's Weird Science

Question: What do spirit photography, after-death weight scales, and psychic research all have in common? Answer: They were all conceived by Boston innovators.

The first spirit photographer was a nineteenth-century engraver and amateur photographer named William Mumler. In 1861, Mr. Mumler posed for a portrait of his own bright-eyed, bushy-bearded self, only to find later, as he hunched over the developing tray, that he hadn't sat in perfect solitude. To his surprise (or so he later maintained), a faint ectoplasmic shape of another figure had magically materialized over his left shoulder.

Mumler went on to replicate this interesting effect, and his output of ghost photographs later drew a large and lucrative clientele. Although Mumler was widely held to be a fraud, he had many supporters who believed that he had stumbled across a genuinely mystifying phenomenon of photography: to wit, the tendency from time to time for anybody's camera to pick up the ghostly shape of a figure invisible to the naked eye. In any event, Mumler's forays into spirit photography coincided with two important cultural influences: the heyday of spiritualism and the Civil War, which left so many Americans bereft and desperate for assurance that their loved ones were not entirely lost to them. The fact that Mumler charged ten dollars apiece for spirit photographs in an age when a normal portrait cost less than a nickel helped fuel skepticism about his motives and methods.

In 1869, Mumler moved his studio from Boston to New York—a mistake it turned out, for almost immediately he was formally charged with fraud, larceny, and obtaining money under false pretenses. In the high-profile trial that ensued, the legitimacy of spirit photography itself was opened up to debate. The defense argued that Mumler had a mediumistic gift. A parade of satisfied customers, who'd identified deceased loved ones in their portraits, was offered up as proof that Mumler provided a valid service. The prosecutor argued that the puffy ghost shapes in Mumler's photos were vague enough to be taken for anyone, and that the bereaved who claimed to recognize departed souls only did so out of a heartbreaking need to believe. In addition, the prosecutor produced darkroom specialists, who explained how spirit subjects could be faked with double exposures or with an even easier trick, a by-product of photography in its infancy. In the early days, a photographic subject was required to sit perfectly still for long minutes while the camera's shutter remained open and the image was recorded. Should a second figure enter the scene (perhaps tiptoeing from behind on bare feet?) and remain for perhaps half a minute, his or her figure would be captured as a pale shimmer, a wisp, a ghost.

The Mumler hearing fed a media frenzy, with front-page newspaper headlines and feature stories in national magazines. The cover of *Harper's Weekly* showcased nine of Mumler's photographs, each a dyad of living and deceased subjects. Finally, the judge dropped all charges, citing a lack of evidence. The *New York Tribune* reported the judge equivocating that "however he might believe that trick and deception had been practiced [by Mumler], yet, as he sat there in his capacity as magistrate, he was compelled to decide . . . [that] the prosecution had failed to prove the case."

Both sides claimed victory, and if the skeptics had thought that by charging Mumler with criminal deeds they could put a stop to spirit photography, they were very much mistaken. Mumler's "art" inspired hosts of imitators, one of whom, William Hope, produced more than 2,500 photos of spirits, about which Troy Taylor of the American Ghost Society recently affirmed on his web site, "I have yet to see one of these photos which appears to be authentic."

The mistake the fakers invariably made was in overproducing the *mise en scène*. Had they studied a few genuine spirit photos (more about that shortly), they would have realized that ghosts appear on the plate as ethereal, nearly transparent outlines, or as perfectly round spheres of light (or darkness) or prismatic dots. The charlatans, in contrast, would use all-too-human models in flowing robes and elaborate headgear. A Parisian photographer named Buguet was discovered to be in possession of hundreds of wigs and costumes in his studio, although he, like Mumler, was accredited by his supporters as being basically legitimate, only resorting to fakery when his occult powers occasionally failed him.

But for all the phonies that have come down the photographic pike in the past hundred and forty-odd years, that doesn't take away from the fact that thousands upon thousands of true spirit photos have been revealed to our astonished eyes and vetted by psychic researchers and photographic experts alike. Some of the most famous are as follows:

The Lord Combermere Photograph was taken in 1891 of the great library of Combermere Abbey in Cheshire, England. To capture the full splendor of the room, the camera was set with an exposure of one full hour. During that time the photographer saw to it that no one entered the library. When the photo was developed the head, body, and arms of Lord Combermere emerged on the print, despite the fact that during that same hour the man in question was being treated to his own funeral at the local churchyard.

In another English graveyard, in 1959, a Mrs. Mabel Chimney photographed her mother's tombstone, then snapped a quick cameo of her husband seated in the passenger seat of their car. Later, the developed print revealed Mrs. Chimney's late mother staring out from the back seat as if to ask, "Are we there yet?" A photo expert from a London newspaper inspected the picture and went on to stake his reputation on its authenticity.

The most famous photo, and one that ends up in every book related to the subject, is known as the Brown Lady of Raynham Hall. In 1936, an Indian photographer named Indre Shira was sent by *Country Life* magazine to take a series of photographs of palatial Raynham Hall in Norfolk, England. He and his assistant had begun to set up their equipment at the base of the grand staircase when Mr. Shira was startled by the sight of "a vapoury form which gradually assumed the shape of a woman in a veil" descending the stairs. The photographer grabbed the camera and hastily took the picture. His assistant, who'd seen nothing on the staircase, had considered his employer temporarily out of his mind ... until he saw the developed photo of a diaphanous shape on the stairs. This was a rare episode of a ghost both seen beforehand and subsequently captured as evidence on film.

In the 1960s, a particularly spooky shot was made by a Reverend K. F. Lord of the altar at England's Newby Church. A black-cowled figure in an ankle-length monk's robe floats over the steps of the altar. The phantom's face is starkly white, with black sockets for eyes, its mouth and jawbone set in the rictus of a long protracted howl. To modern viewers, the resemblance to the diabolical serial killer in the *Scream* movies is unmistakable and upsetting.

Closer to home, there are very few of us who haven't received a roll of developed prints back from the camera store without puzzling over an occasional strange photograph—a diffusion of lights perhaps, without any known source, or a bubble bath of white spheres, believed by many psychic researchers to be ectoplasmic in origin. Often reasonable explanations put our minds at rest, but other times we're left wondering. Many of these "mishaps" occur at a site where some sort of haunting has been suspected, and we have to ask ourselves why, on the same roll of film, taken by the same camera on the same day, the photos of Aunt Becky's birthday party are perfectly clear, while at the alleged ghost spot those sizzles of pale lavender light keep cropping up.

Whatever William Mumler's intent in bringing spirit photography to public attention, he unleashed generations of heirs who've struggled, some larcenously, some sincerely, with this particular artistic form of technology crossed with the supernatural. And since nearly every one of us owns a camera, we are all invited to explore this realm of the unknowable— made just the sheerest bit tangible.

In 1906, another Boston man of science, Dr. Duncan Mac-Dougall, offered intriguing proof that the soul has substance. Of course, any serious theologian would argue that the soul exists with or without a quantifiable measurement—that's what's called faith—but Dr. MacDougall hoped to enlarge our understanding of spirit, as opposed to flesh, by showing that spirit has its own infinitesimal "flesh." In short, he sought to slap the soul down on a scale the way a fishmonger weighs cod, but with a bit more finesse.

At Boston's Massachusetts General Hospital, Dr. Mac-

Dougall constructed a bed frame over a system of scales so finely calibrated they could measure weight to a tenth of an ounce. Next, he sought volunteers whose chief qualification had to be that they were dying. His preference was for terminal souls so wrung with exhaustion they'd be less disposed to last minute twitches and spasms that might jockey the scales. Tuberculosis deaths, of which there were many, perfectly suited his purposes.

The doctor budgeted for substances escaping from the body, such as air from the lungs, and then in the micromoment of a patient's death, he peered at the scales for a final resolution. In every case, the body in that instant lost several measurable ounces. For example, in the following typical case study, Dr. MacDougall wrote, "At the end of three hours and forty minutes [the patient] expired, and suddenly, coincident with death, the beam end dropped with an audible stroke, hitting against the lower limiting bar and remaining there with no rebound."

Dr. MacDougall and many parapsychologists who've encountered his work were convinced an extra step had been taken toward our greater understanding of afterlife materiality. Or to paraphrase Descartes, "I weigh, therefore I am."

A Bostonian who brought respect to the study of paranormal events was the distinguished philosopher and psychologist William James (brother to the famous novelist Henry James). From 1872 to 1907 William James taught at Harvard (first physiology and anatomy, then psychology and philosophy). His speaking style was so riveting, his ideas so innovative, that he packed his lecture halls to standing-room-only capacity. His *Principles of Psychology,* published in 1890, launched on American soil the exciting new field of psychoanalysis. *The Will to Believe* (1897) and *The Varieties of Religious Experience* (1902) are still widely read today for their insights into spiritual questing. *Pragmatism* (1907) launched a whole new trend of thought in intellectual circles.

In the 1880s James trained his sights on the new parapsychologies springing up around him—spirit photography, table rapping, mediumship, etc.—and he moved to subject the phenomena to scientific scrutiny. If any of it could pass the test of the most objective, empirical analysis, well then, some pretty amazing mysteries would come to light! The upshot was the American Society for Psychical Research, cofounded by James in Boston in 1885 and later relocated to New York. The professor's sponsorship brought the stamp of approval to the enterprise.

One of James's most notable inquiries concerned a Boston medium named Leonora Piper. This woman of modest background struck all who met her as a person possessed of true psychic powers. Although Professor James was a natural skeptic, which lent authority to his final pronouncements, he came to believe that, among all the fakes, Mrs. Piper was the genuine article. Flashier mediums produced loud rapping and theatrical illusions, whereas Mrs. Piper settled into a trance that suspended her beyond the domain of the material world. In the spirit dimension, she had various guides: J.S. Bach, an Indian girl named Chlorine, Cornelius Vanderbilt, Henry Wadsworth Longfellow, actress Sarah Siddons, and a rude, crude Frenchman named Dr. Phinuit. From these controls and others, Mrs. Piper conveyed messages from the dead. In every generation a medium comes along (today we have a number of them, such as John Edward, Sylvia Browne, and George Anderson) who astounds the living with information that only they and their deceased loved ones could have possibly known, along the lines of, "Your amber-bead necklace fell down behind the liquor cabinet in the library," or, "Tell Clara I'm sorry I forgot her birthday on our trip to Marblehead." Mrs. Piper's communiqués from the Other Side were so convincing, they led William James to famously proclaim: "If you wish to upset the law that all crows are black, you must not seek to show that no crows are: It is enough that you prove one single crow to be white. My own white crow is Mrs. Piper. In the trances of this medium, I cannot resist the conviction that knowledge appears which she never gained by the ordinary waking use of her eyes and ears and wits."

James's allusion to a white crow was adopted by another psychical group, the ghost-hunting White Crow Society, headquartered in Hillsdale, N.J., which to this day specializes in domestic exorcisms. Whatever nuisance homeowners need swept from their dwellings—demons, poltergeists, or unlovable ghosts—the White Crow Society escorts these supernatural pests to a more appropriate place.

So, who ya gonna call? Well, in addition to the White Crow Society, there are also the International Ghost Hunter's Society, the Catholic Archdiocese's exorcist division, as well as assorted individuals scattered across the country with experience and expertise in this tricky arena. Thanks to the interest of important thinkers such as William James, the entire field has achieved the impossible—credibility!

✠ 10 ✠

Goodbyes from the Back of Beyond

The occult phenomenon perhaps dearest to all our hearts is the possibility of communicating with a departed loved one. In Boston in the fall of 2000, psychic James Van Praag lectured on the subject to a packed house in the cathedral-sized sanctuary of the Unitarian Universalist Church on Boylston Street. For six hours (with a noon break for lunch), Mr. Van Praag received specific messages from the otherworld, drawing forth squeals of recognition from members of the audience:"Is there a Paul here? I'm getting a reference to a red bicycle and a ride from Sandwich to Chatham when you got caught in the rain."

A provocative anecdote was related by author S. Ralph Harlow, a former professor of theology at Harvard, in his book *Life After Death*, published in the 1960s. He and his younger sister, in their growing up years, had nourished a strong interest in all matters mystical, and particularly in what awaited them in the next world. In early adulthood the siblings made a pact that whoever predeceased the other would transmit from beyond the grave a "clear-cut signal" of continued consciousness. "We were both very definite about the terminology," wrote Dr. Harlow,"reminding each other that it had to be

CLEAR CUT." Throughout their twenties, the Harlows re-minded each other of the plan. They never expected to launch the experiment in the short term, but, tragically, Ralph's sister died suddenly in her early thirties. In the first days of grief and shock, Ralph forgot about their pact.

Some days after the funeral, Dr. Harlow was sitting in a fog of bereavement in his office, struggling to keep up with the eager philosophical chatter of a coed student seated across from him. The professor's desk was empty of all but a con-ventional glass paperweight that had been in his possession so long he barely noticed it. All of a sudden, as if struck by an unseen mallet, the paperweight split down the middle with a crack loud enough to make both teacher and student jump in their seats. A moment later they heard the unmistakable inflections of Ralph's sister's voice: *"Is that clear cut enough for you?"*

Teacher and student stared around them at the empty air, then gaped at the paperweight resting in two separate wedges on the shiny mahogany desk. Without a word, the coed rose from her chair and fled the room. She never again sought a private conference.

Here's another one: A Boston businessman named Robert B. reported intriguing incidents following the death of both his parents. An only child, Robert had been close to his mother, so it was with an aching heart on an evening in the spring of 1986 that he took his leave from her as she clung to life in a city hospital. He stooped to kiss her forehead and told her he'd see her in the morning.

"Yes, you will," she whispered.

He returned to his apartment and, retreating from sorrow, sank into a deep sleep. Past midnight he was awakened by a buzzing sound in his room. His first thought was that a hive of bees had taken up residence inside his walls. He opened his eyes to see a luminous cloud drift into his room from the hallway. The cloud swept over him, twinkling, then swooshed out the window in wisps of light that flattened to meet the cracks of the Venetian blinds.

The next morning, he learned that his mother had died.

Five years later, Robert's father passed away in the same hospital. Although fully grown (as he'd been when his mother died), Robert felt orphaned. His father's death reopened wounds incurred at his mother's passing, so that he grieved doubly. Again alone in his apartment, he lay awake, unable to nod off even for a minute. Suddenly, from across the room, he heard the unmistakable sounds of typing, reminding him that his mother had taught secretarial skills at a local high school. That signature noise was followed by the familiar sound of his dad whistling "Mack the Knife." Robert bolted up in bed, and as he did so, a luminous cloud billowed out from the wall. It massed itself into a two-pronged shape like a plowshare, then streamed toward him, passing through his body. He felt a wave of static electricity sizzling from head to toe and out through his fingertips. "Dad!" he cried out. The cloud swirled over his head and discharged itself through the ceiling.

At his father's funeral, Robert found a basket of white-silk irises among the fresh lilies, roses, and carnations sent by friends and family. No tag accompanied the silk flowers, and he culled them from the fresh blooms, tossing the bouquet in the back seat of his Toyota. After the interment, during the drive home, he began to notice a disagreeable odor. "It was the smell of death," he said, "and I thought I was imagining it and therefore going slightly bonkers." He found a parking spot in front of his apartment, and automatically grabbed the basket of artificial flowers as he exited his car. He brought them upstairs, depositing them on a side table in his foyer. A couple of hours later, he realized the foul smell he'd detected in the car now permeated his apartment. Immediately he knew the stench came from the silk flowers, although, strangely, when he stooped to sniff them, they had no apparent odor. None-theless, he hustled the basket downstairs and tucked it in a corner of the small entryway between the street door and the communicating door.

An hour later he received a phone call from the building manager. "I heard your father died—sorry," the man said brusquely. "Are those your flowers in the entryway? I had to toss 'em in the trash out back. Got complaints from other tenants comin' home tonight, and I figured it had to be the flowers, though I never knew a fake flower to smell one way or the other!"

The next day Robert checked with the mortuary to see whether an employee had recorded receipt of the artificial irises. It turned out the memento had been sent by a man who Robert's father believed had swindled him in a business deal. Robert concluded that the "swindler" hadn't deliberately in-fused the flowers with stench, although he thought the artifi-cial blossoms to be in questionable taste. "I had the feeling my father's spirit saturated the flowers with a symbolic essence of the man's character. And he wanted to make sure they ended up where they belonged—in the dumpster! I only hope it did-n't make the alley smell any worse than usual!"

During the course of a parapsychologist's fieldwork, the caseload of tales of goodbyes from departed loved ones is large and eminently reassuring. In grief, we long for proof of a prevailing spirit, and even the piquant possibility that we'll meet again in a better, or at least another, place. The more we delve for stories of this nature, the more convinced we become that "clear-cut signals" abound. As James Van Praag wrote in his best-selling book *Talking to Heaven*, "When someone passes over, he or she does not stop thinking of you. The love bond created on earth continues in the spirit world."

The Wail of the Banshee

Those who've heard the howl of a banshee live in dread of encountering it ever again. Some describe it as a series of high-pitched shrieks with the rise and fall of a gale-force wind. Others say the banshee's cry is like the scream of something inhuman, a berserk demon. And there are those who have likened the wail of the banshee to the sobs of a bereft mother in the first outpouring of her grief, a sound that cuts to the listener's heart and soul. All who've heard it have maintained that, although less than human, the banshee's wail also sounds unlike anything found in the animal kingdom. Generally, it starts low, grows to an unbearable pitch, then fades, as if slowly and painfully reeled back to the nether world.

The myth of the banshee originated long ago in Ireland in pagan, pre-Christian times. Normally we think of the first big wave of Irish settlers flocking to American shores in 1848, during the devastating potato famine. In certain pockets of academia, however, scholars believe another Irish influx may have taken place centuries earlier. Stonehenge-type structures in North Salem, Massachusetts, and New Hampshire, and beehive-shaped shrines all over the East, suggest that Irish Culdee monks colonized New England in the fourth century

A.D. They may have imported, if not actual banshees, then certainly the legend of them.

The legend is as follows: A personal spirit—a depressing guardian, to be sure—attaches itself to a family and comes to warn it of impending death. If the banshee believes it's doing anyone a favor, it should think again. Clearly we would all prefer to pass away, or see our relatives pass away, in peace rather than have the event presaged with a long, loud, ululating lament that strikes terror into the hearts of all listeners. The word *banshee* comes from *ban sidhe*, which in Gaelic means "fairy woman." She's been depicted as everything from a red-haired maiden in a flowing gray cloak to a frightful crone over twelve feet tall whose black cape shimmers and swirls with the velocity of a cyclone.

Even more hideous than the banshee is the *bean-nighe*, or Little-Washer-by-the-Stream. This unhappy creature is apparently the ghost of a woman who died during childbirth, and is forced to wash clothes in a river until the time comes when the woman would have passed away of natural causes. The clothes churning in the water are bloody and believed to signify an imminent death in the community. Unlike the *ban sidhe* of the red hair, who, though you wish she'd shut up, is graceful and lovely, the *bean-nighe* is a beast from Hell with one nostril, one front tooth, withered breasts, and webbed feet.

The fact that the banshee is specific to Irish lore may cast doubt on its authenticity. When it comes to proving the existence of anything less tangible than, say, a bowl of oatmeal or a toad on a hydrangea leaf, we rely on universality. There is probably no culture on the planet that doesn't have a body of literature about ghosts, witches, angels, and demons. The myth of the vampire, too, pervades most societies, including some of the remotest tribes. But banshees? If the Irish alone dreamed them up, then perhaps the Average Non-Irish Joe stands as much chance of hearing a banshee's wail as having a leprechaun dance a jig on his knee.

But it could also be argued that the collective consciousness of a tribe of people produces its own weird reality. Our minds can wrestle into being miraculous shapes, sounds, and smells. Hence, the Passamaquoddy Indians had their *Nagumwasuck,* medieval Russians their *upir,* and ancient Celts their *ban sidhe.* And who is to say that when these spectral figures appeared to their peoples they weren't, in their own indefinable way, absolutely real?

A particular banshee story has for decades been an article of faith to residents of Boston. In the 1960s a successful businessman came forward with an unforgettable story. Although he declined to furnish his name, he was perfectly forthcoming about his family background. In the mid-nineteenth century his Irish Catholic ancestors, refugees of the potato famine, had arrived in Boston. His great-great-grandfather opened a mom-and-pop grocery store, which eventually flourished into a chain of supermarkets. For this family, in other words, it was just a hop, skip, and a jump from Southie to Beacon Hill.

The teller of the story was ten years old when he first heard the banshee. On a sunny spring morning, the chirping of birds outside his window nudged him from sleep. Suddenly he heard a low, keening noise, like a rising wind. The noise intensified, annihilating the birdsong. It sounded like a frantic sobbing, a "demented woman," as he described it years later. Anxiously he gazed out the window. Not a breath of wind stirred. And there was no demented woman, or anyone else for that matter, in sight.

The boy fled downstairs, but there he came upon a distressing scene. His father sat in his armchair, arms propped on his knees, head in hands, weeping unreservedly. The boy's mother explained: they had just received news that the boy's grandfather had died only minutes before.

At the time, the boy hadn't connected the death with the horrifying wail. No one had ever related to him the myth of the banshee; for the most part the lore had been left behind in the Old World. But a few years later the boy heard the tale of the banshee's dire warning and immediately remembered the mysterious cry portending news of his grandpa's death.

In 1946 the banshee returned. The boy was now a young man, an air force officer stationed in Asia. Once again the *ban sidhe* arrived in the morning, jolting him from sleep. This time he knew what it meant, and stark terror seized him. As he wrote decades later, "I sat bolt upright in bed, and the hair on the back of my neck prickled. The noise got louder, rising and falling like an air raid siren."

At last the howl faded, leaving in its place a great sadness. The young man knew with that prescience that binds us to our nearest and dearest that his father had passed away. In a matter of hours his fear was confirmed.

In twelve years' time the Boston supermarket mogul found himself in Toronto on business. Again it was morning, and again he lay in bed, although on this occasion he was fully awake and reading a newspaper. Suddenly, from under the eaves of the hotel windows, a series of low moans issued into the room. The man cast the paper aside and stared in horror at the source of the sound. The moans escalated to shrill cries of lamentation. Covering his ears, the man looked frantically around, as if he could escape the awful portent.

At last the shrieks subsided, then stopped. In the silence the man tried to keep panic at bay. Had the banshee cried for his wife? His young son? His brothers? Several hurried phone calls assured him that all was well within his family.

In a couple of hours, he emerged from the elevator into the hotel lobby and heard the day's breaking news. At once he knew for whom the banshee had howled: It was November 22, 1963. His boyhood friend, John F. Kennedy, another Irish lad from Boston who'd become president of the United States, had been slain by an assassin.

PART IV

Haunted Landmarks

Beacon Street, showing Boston Athenaeum, c. 1875

There are some who opine
that every major Boston landmark is haunted.
Picture some of them: the Public Library,
with its Greek Revival arches and megalithic stones;
the State House, topped by a million-watt gold dome;
Copp's Burying Ground in the North End,
its tombstones blasted by British artillery fire.
If these places aren't haunted, then neither is
the Roman Forum or Versailles (which we know
to be famously phantomed). But we haven't
time to cover all of Boston's ectoplasmic hot spots,
so we'll concentrate on the following . . . ⇥

⤝ 12 ⤞

Who Walks Charlesgate Hall's Halls?

The magnificent Gilded Age palace known as Charlesgate Hall is Boston's Dakota. You know the Dakota: the New York landmark that rises above Central Park like a brooding castle from the mists of Camelot; the setting for *Rosemary's Baby*. Like the Dakota of that famous film, Charlesgate Hall has had its share of satanic cults, but we're getting ahead of the story ...

In 1891, for the sum of $170,000, construction began on a 14,000-square-foot lot at 4 Charlesgate, just off Beacon Street in the Back Bay area. With six stories of dark brick, bay windows, and medieval turrets spiking the roof line, the Charlesgate Hotel resembled a quaint version of London's Parliament building, flanked by six thousand square feet of gardens. The inside was no less sumptuous: the foyer gleamed with exquisite Grueby tiles; ceilings soared; archways vaulted; and marble, mosaics, wrought-iron filigree, and bas-reliefs presided everywhere, and baronial fireplaces warmed the rooms.

The architect, J. Pickering Putnam, made no bones about the fact that the residential hotel was designed for luxury seekers of the topmost drawer. He even had a bit of a crusade going: in architectural journals he described the emerging chateau at 4 Charlesgate as Modern (Rich) Man's answer to the angst of living in isolated dwellings. Square foot for square foot and dollar for dollar, he demonstrated how much added value derived from living in what was coming to be known as the "French flat," the "Continental" or the "Family Hotel." In the in-town single family dwelling that he called a "tower," rooms had to be tightly packed one on top of the other; whereas with the flat, you could spread them out, incorporating grander elements of design and style. By sharing a central dining room downstairs, one could eliminate the clutter of redundant kitchen facilities as well as lodging for a private cook and other help.

As a matter of fact, part of Mr. Putnam's mission was to liberate his wealthy clients from the annoyance of unnecessary staff. In his own words:

> In the "tower" life is spent in training and treating with servants, mechanics and marketmen. The private cook is a volcano in a house, slumbering at times, but always ready to burst forth into destructive eruption. True repose is out of the question, and we are told that the motive for foreign travel of perhaps one half of Americans is rest from household cares and the enjoyment of good attendance, freed from any responsibility of its organization and management.

Rich people of the world, arise and throw off your shackles!

So perhaps more than any other luxe apartment complex of the time, the Charlesgate was responsible for shoehorning the upper classes out of their independent mansions and into French flat living. Putnam himself resided there with his family until his death in 1917. The cachet of grandeur clung to the Boston palace as names from the social register studded the directory clear up until 1947, when the property was sold to Boston University for use as a dormitory.

It wasn't until its later incarnation as another college's residence hall that the Charlesgate overflowed with occult happenings, but even during BU's tenure, several spooky stories came to light: In the early 1970s, in a sixth-floor chamber that had supposedly been the site of a suicide, an alarm clock frequently buzzed at 6:11 a.m. without anyone setting it for that time. Also on the sixth floor, three freshmen girls moved into one of the rooms to find themselves accosted by the spirit world. The first to arrive decided to stake out the larger of the two closets, but when she placed her hand on the knob, she felt a sudden aversion to opening the door. She opted for the other closet. The second girl to enter the room also approached the larger closet, experienced the same unease, and suggested they leave it for the third roommate. Later all three girls—presumably after the third had in turn rejected the off-putting closet—made a startling discovery: the year before, a student had hanged herself in the larger closet.

In 1972, when BU sold the building, room 623 was found to be boarded up. It appeared that two years earlier a male freshman had slept alone in the room. He awoke one night to the outrageous sight of a man floating above his bed. He let loose a series of screams, and the resident advisor on the floor charged down the corridor to investigate. Barreling into the room to reprimand the student, he was brought up short by the spectacle of a man suspended over the freshman's bed. There was no disputing the RA's corroborating testimony; the room was vacated and permanently sealed.

The period between 1972 and 1981, before Emerson College purchased 4 Charlesgate, marks the shadiest portion of the building's history. The developer holding the deed to the property was generally portrayed as a slumlord. The grand old structure had certainly begun to look like a tenement, with pigeon droppings on window sills, dirt galore, flats broken up into a warren of dingy rooms, stairways dark with aged varnish, rusted pipes, an archaic electrical system, and, most flagrantly alarming, a rear elevator so faulty that complaints about it were recorded as far back as the early 1920s.

Over the years a number of accidents had occurred in the elevator, including one in the 1930s, when the hoist cables snapped, plunging five ladies and the operator eleven feet to the ground floor. Those occupants were unhurt, but another time the passenger wasn't so lucky: In December 1941 the doors opened for a young woman who strode into the elevator shaft and fell six floors. She was taken to a hospital, where she subsequently died. (Oddly enough, students at Charlesgate Hall over the years often reported dreaming of hospital gurneys slowly rolling past them in the corridors. This led to speculation that the building had once been a hospital—a false notion, but possibly the elevator-accident victim returned on occasion to broadcast visions of her last memories on earth.) In any event, the rear elevator never properly responded to repairs, and for nearly fifty years it sat boarded up and abandoned, lending another spine-tingling touch to the already creepy premises.

During the nine "flophouse" years, the owner of the Charlesgate reserved some of the rooms for dormitory living, leased to various colleges, and rented the remainder to adult tenants. The dormitory trade allowed him to skirt regulations for rent control, which would otherwise have applied to the rooming house. The most questionable side of this arrangement was the extent to which students were exposed to other residents, and not just your average neighbors, but (according to the written testimony of several students) devil-worshipping cultists! Freshmen maintained that they sometimes spied through open doors a cluster of black-garbed celebrants chanting around a black pentagram painted on the floor, backlit by candles. To each his own, of course, but in the later Emerson College years many people attributed dark events at the Charlesgate to evil spirits conjured up by all this pentagram action.

In 1981, after purchasing the property, the Emerson College trustees poured a million dollars into renovating its tired rooms. And in spite of its decline during the slumlord era, the building retained some of its old glories. As one of the workmen at the time exclaimed while showing a newspaper reporter around the place, "This is my chapel. Look at the dome overhead and the woodwork on the ceiling. The fireplace is marble. . . . Look at the tapered columns and the fluted pilasters. The wood is all mahogany and oak. You don't find anything like this unless you go to Italy or France."

And so a fresh brigade of students moved into Charlesgate Hall in the late 1980s, and whatever spirits had been mustering forces for the past nine decades now blew through the rooms with the force of the strange winds that sometimes gusted along the corridors.

"It was September 27, 1987, 3 a.m.," wrote freshman Cindy Ludlow to Emerson College archivist Robert Fleming. Referring to herself in the third person she noted, "She was sleeping on the bottom bunk and her roommate was gone for the weekend." Ludlow went on to describe how she was awakened by sounds of commotion. She felt the edge of her mattress flatten as if someone were stepping onto it to hoist herself up to the upper bunk. The bed frame jounced and shook, and Cindy heard sheets and blankets rustling. She turned on the light and checked the upper bunk. There was no one there. "She left the room for the rest of the night. The next morning she came back to the room and noticed that the top bunk which had been made was rumpled and the sheets were pulled back."

Archivist Robert Fleming encouraged the residents of Charlesgate Hall to share their experiences and contribute written affidavits to the archives. Although he himself is no great believer in the paranormal, he admits he's been persuaded, by the sheer volume of stories, that something in the realm of the unexplainable was, in fact, going on. He also preferred to take an open approach with the students rather than have them suspect a coverup. Before Fleming's tenure, a rumor had circulated that a secret file on the Charlesgate ghosts was tucked away in Boston's Public Library, but that officials of Emerson College had forced the library to seal the documents. Rather than see the dormitory turn into Boston's Roswell, Fleming permitted the students their say.

One of the more interesting cases was published in the journal *FATE* by a sophomore named Tracey Libby. As she submitted her report on September 4, 1988, she asserted, "All names, except for the author, have been changed for privacy. They are on file at the *FATE* office. All have sworn on a notarized statement that this story—amazing as it sounds— is true."

Libby described an evening in October 1987 when she and four other dorm mates, one boy and three girls, decided to while away a Saturday night by using a Ouija board to probe the source of the Charlesgate mysteries. They met in Mary's room. "Everyone took turns, but nothing frightening took place until Mary and Josh got to the board. That was when the phone rang." Mary answered, listened for a moment, looked startled, then carried the phone in the hallway to continue the conversation.

When she returned she told them her father had called and that he knew they were using the Ouija board: "He's psychic. He said that he had seen a red flag signaling danger. We've opened a psychic window letting evil spirits through." On nervous looks from her friends, she went on to explain,

"My father said that we must close the window as soon as possible. I don't know how to do it, but we've got to try. This is serious stuff, guys."

The five students decided to take the board downstairs to the common room, as no one wanted to unleash evil spirits in private quarters. They endured a harrowing few hours of dialogue with the board. Several entities vied for attention. One, called "Mama," was purely malevolent, but at last another, kinder spirit assured the students that the window had been closed.

Other students experienced disturbing interactions with Ouija boards. Sophomore Mike D'Alonzo moved out of the Charlesgate into an apartment on Beacon Street after a rude encounter of his own: In the sixth-floor lounge, he and a friend, using a Ouija board, contacted a spirit named DLD. All of a sudden, "glass was flying everywhere," according to D'Alonzo. As other students entered the room, DLD furnished surprisingly personal information about them. The questioners asked the spirit whether he resided on the premises. DLD answered in the affirmative, citing his specific room as D'Alonzo's!

Was it any wonder that school officials banned the use of Ouija boards in Charlesgate Hall? (This didn't, however, prevent curious students from bootlegging an occasional session.)

In the fall of 1986, a student named Jamie Kagiliery strolled down the hallway of the sixth floor and, rounding the corner, came upon a man dressed in black: "black pants, black coat, boots, even a strange black hat." The man slipped into the men's bathroom, and the door glided shut behind him. Kagiliery felt uneasy, but he followed the person into the bathroom: "I pretend I'm washing my hands as I glance under both of the stalls. No man! I rush to the showers and throw open the curtain. Still no man. I'm alone in the room!"

Kagiliery entered into the records another story about a

girl living on the third floor. She'd just moved into her room and brought from home a musical elephant windup toy. She unpacked it and twisted the tiny knob, but when she placed the elephant on her bed table, it sat silent and unbudging. Shrugging, she moved along to her next item, a tape recorder, popped in a cassette, and pressed "play." The tape deck did nothing, but the musical elephant immediately chimed out its nursery rhyme! Astonished, the girl pressed the "stop" button on the tape recorder. The elephant switched off. Many more times she tested the strange crossed signals between her tape recorder and the music box. Without fail the buttons on the tape deck activated the ceramic elephant. She requested a room change and, once installed elsewhere, the two items functioned normally.

In the November 1982 issue of the student newspaper, *The Berkeley Beacon,* two residents of the second floor of Charlesgate Hall, Liz Durkin and Donna Capaldi, related their own creepy experiences. One night Durkin awoke and heard a rustling from Capaldi's bed on the opposite wall. She glanced over to see her roommate sound asleep, but her covers were undulating half a foot above her body. Squinching her eyes shut and trying to will herself back to sleep, Liz then heard a disembodied voice utter her name.

Some weeks later, Durkin's sister, Kelly, arrived for Parents Weekend. The younger sister shared the dorm mates' room, and she woke up in the wee hours of Sunday morning to announce, "A ghost was just in me!" The possession had manifested itself in severe chills, a roiling stomach, and a sensation of wind blowing through her hair.

In the same year a girl named Laura Douglas found herself alone one Tuesday night at 10:00 in the laundry room. As she folded her clothes, she felt a tap on her shoulder. She spun around, but there was no one in the room with her. She hurriedly finished her chore but again felt a tap on her shoulder.

She gathered up her clothes, heard a noise like a footstep, and felt the tap once more. This time she glanced at her shoulder and saw an indentation in the foam of her shoulder pad, as if someone meant to restrain her from leaving. She fled the room.

Another young woman reported an incident involving a group of friends in a room of the Charlesgate wing called the Mansion. All of a sudden, the door banged shut and the lights switched off. Unseen forces slammed the students about in the dark. When the lights flooded back on, the terrified girls saw that the walls and ceilings were now gouged and scarred. The girls stampeded from the room, convinced they'd been visited by evil.

The stories are endless, many of them concerning glasses sliding across tables; room temperatures plunging to thirty degrees; doors spontaneously shutting and locking; blankets plucked from sleeping students; and students awakening far from their beds, on the floor, shivering with cold.

A note regarding the historical facts behind these hauntings: there are none. Over the years, students and journalists have attributed the Charlesgate ghosts to unholy numbers of murders and suicides having taken place in the building. In fact, no newspaper accounts exist for any shady events; however, after eleven decades, during which thousands of tenants have churned through the building's halls, it's a statistical probability that at least a few murders and suicides occurred. In the days when the social elite ruled the Charlesgate directory, it required no more than a phone call or a word in the ear of a fellow resident to wrap ultimate discretion around a corpse trundled from the building via the service entrance. And if murders were easy to cover up, suicides were an even simpler matter to obscure; even today, coroners seem happier to attribute death to accident or irreversible disorder.

In any event, by the early 1990s the Emerson College era

at Charlesgate Hall was drawing to a close. Perhaps because the ghostly manifestations appeared to be veering out of control, or more prosaically because the college required its students to move closer to its new campus along the southeastern corner of Boston Commons, the trustees sold the Charlesgate in 1994 to a private developer. The edifice, still magnificent after all these years, has "gone condo." Thus far no new ghost stories have come to light.

Whatever's happening at 4 Charlesgate nowadays, it's clear that the golden age of its haunting occurred during the High Dorm years of 1981 to 1994. All that postadolescent energy combined with ghosts and the building's turbulent history to create an occult combustion almost beyond belief. It's arguably a blessing that landmark has been put to rest as a dormitory: most students would prefer that the challenges of college life remained strictly academic.

⟞ 13 ⟝

What Nathaniel Hawthorne Saw

Does it surprise us that a famous author of gothic horror should experience the real deal firsthand? In 1851 Nathaniel Hawthorne published his disquieting and melancholy novel, *The House of the Seven Gables.* The brooding manor house of the title, half timber, half plaster, was built in Salem, Massachusetts, and the region's earlier bleak history (see Chapter 25) hovered over the dwelling.

As background for the novel, one Colonel Pyncheon had stolen a plot of land from Matthew Maule by the simple expedient of having the poor man executed as a warlock. Before he died, Maule levied a curse that God would give Pyncheon and his descendants blood to drink. By the time the novel's action unfolds, three Pyncheons of three generations have expired in the same great oak chair, choked to death on blood that stained their shirtfronts scarlet. Hawthorne based the character of Matthew Maule on the case—and curse—of Giles Corey, one of the victims of the Salem Witchcraft Trials of 1692. And the seven-gabled manor house does indeed exist in Salem as a museum, delighting visitors to this now picturesque seaport town.

Several years before Nathaniel Hawthorne sat down to

write *The House of the Seven Gables,* he had a remarkable ghostly experience of his own that played itself out day after day for several weeks. Fans of Hawthorne's writing have conjectured that this brush with the supernatural helped to inspire the uneasy mysticism woven into the fabric of his novel.

The Boston Athenaeum, a private library and club, was founded in 1807. The august facility now occupies five stories of resplendent Renaissance-style sandstone at 10½ Beacon Street, but up until 1847 it was housed at 13 Pearl Street. It was there, in 1842, that the thirty-six-year-old Hawthorne occupied the members-only reading room, passing hours—sometimes entire work days—engrossed in newspapers, books, and all manner of research materials. During this time, another fixture of the reading room was a distinguished Unitarian minister, Dr. Thaddeus Harris. The reverend and the author rarely spoke; both men honored the solitary nature of literary pursuits that renders libraries silent as monasteries. Still, they exchanged the common courtesy of nodding at one another across the soundproofing length of a Persian carpet. Daily, without any variation in his routine, the elderly cleric sat in an armchair beside the fire, immersing himself in the *Boston Post* as if all the secrets of the universe were contained in its pages.

Hawthorne described Dr. Harris as a "small, withered, infirm, but brisk old gentleman, with snow-white hair, a somewhat stooping figure, but yet a remarkable alacrity of movement." One day the author settled in the reading room with a small stack of journals and glanced, in passing, at the reassuring figure of the old minister seated by the fire. As time ticked by, Hawthorne began to feel as if he were under intense scrutiny. He looked up to see the old gent staring at him with a look of uncommon intensity. Later that evening, at a local restaurant, a friend of Hawthorne's asked if he'd heard the news that Dr. Thaddeus Harris had died. Hawthorne recollected: "'No', said I very quietly, 'and it cannot be true, for I saw him at the Athenaeum today.'"

During the course of the evening and the following morning, Hawthorne received confirmation from other sources that the Unitarian minister had, indeed, passed away, and Hawthorne assumed the event had taken place after Harris had left the club that very afternoon.

He felt a pang of regret that his routine in the reading room would henceforth be missing one of its comforting features. The following morning, as he entered the great hall of the Athenaeum, he mulled over these sad thoughts before climbing the stairs to his favorite nook. "As I opened the door of the reading room, I glanced toward the spot and chair where Dr. Harris usually sat, and there to my astonishment sat the gray, infirm figure of the deceased Doctor, reading the newspaper as was his wont."

Hawthorne pulled himself together, seated himself in his usual place, and dove into his work. When others entered the room, he lifted his gaze to observe how they reacted to the presence of the late minister. No one else seemed to notice Dr. Harris, and Hawthorne could think of no way to bring— tactfully and sanely—the specter to their attention. And the specter, for his part, seemed equally impervious to them, though he persisted in his usual aloof connection to Hawthorne, nodding at him from across the room and occasionally treating the author to that same brief, fevered stare.

What later surprised Hawthorne was how quickly he adjusted to the bizarre situation. For several weeks following Dr. Harris's death, the author continued to share a daily companionable silence with the deceased clergyman across the carpeted floor of the reading room. In time Hawthorne may have regretted missing an opportunity to explore life's greatest unknown. What would have happened, after all, if he'd approached Dr. Harris and asked, "So, what's it like to be dead?"

But for the duration of those weeks the author moved in a cloud of strangely numb disinterest. The sight of the minister "grew to be so common that at length I regarded the venerable defunct no more than any of the other old fogies who basked before the fire and dozed over their newspapers." Later he speculated on his lack of excitement: "Perhaps after all I had a secret dread of the old phenomenon and therefore kept within my limits with a secret caution which I mistook for indifference." In other words, he was frightened enough to retreat into a condition of mild catalepsy!

Nathaniel Hawthorne wasn't the last visitor to the Athenaeum to learn that the venerable institution, whether at Pearl Street or Beacon Street, is supremely haunted. The club's post-1847 home on Beacon Street may be even more riddled with spirit life than was its predecessor, thanks in part to the fact that the south side of the Athenaeum looms above the Granary Burial Ground. While the burial ground itself is not apparently haunted, its inherent potential for otherworldly activity seems to have leached into the neighboring building.

The library is accessible to visitors, who may stroll through the first and second floors to admire the lofty architecture and distinguished art collection. The public is barred, however, from using the haunted elevator, which rises and falls of its own accord as if prankish spirits amuse themselves by flitting in and out of the cabin, pushing buttons for all five floors. According to Boston ghost hunter Jim McCabe, thousands of dollars have been poured into fixing the elevator's unending glitches, to no avail. McCabe commented, "A director at the Athenaeum told me they're throwing in the towel and going for a brand-new elevator," as part of massive renovations of the entire building in 2001–2002. It remains to be seen whether the trouble will persist. After all, it wouldn't be the first time technology proved helpless against the whims of a few dedicated spooks.

Students of the paranormal are apt to wonder whether the Reverend Thaddeus Harris has anything to do with the haunting of the Beacon Street facility. It's rare but not unknown for a ghost to pack up and move with its living roommates when a change of address occurs. A tantalizing hint lies in the fact that when the Beacon Street elevator acted up, it concluded each phantom cycle by stopping and opening its doors on the second-floor foyer, which just happens to be dominated by a portrait of the long-dead minister.

Staff members at the Athenaeum are reluctant to speak of their encounters with in-dwelling spirits. "Well, of course, strange things happen here," confided one official, who prefers to pass into the record unnamed. And he added, "Yes, we've had problems with the elevator, but we expect all will be in good working order when we reopen in June of 2002." Good luck! Most paranormalists know that nothing disgruntles a ghost—or a commune of ghosts—so much as a major redo!

⤛ 14 ⤜

Bodies, Bodies Everywhere

You can tell a great city by its fascinating cemeteries. Boston certainly has its share, one of which is notably haunted.

The Central Burying Ground sits on the south side of Boston Common, along Boylston Street. The cemetery is old enough for most of its inmates' identities to be lost or otherwise unknown, but legend has it that heroes from the Battle of Bunker Hill repose there, as well as British soldiers who died of privations suffered during the Siege of Boston. Colonial portrait painter Gilbert Stuart rests at the site, as does Mary Dyer, celebrated early Quaker and victim of Puritan prejudice. Graves marked "Stranger" refer to Irish Catholic immigrants. In early American graveyards such as this one, the tombstones face east, the better to prepare for Judgment Day, and the small footstones at the end of each mound mark off a natural bed for final sleep.

On a drizzly afternoon in the 1970s, a dentist named Dr. Matt Rutger decided to wander in the tranquil beauty of the ancient graveyard and encountered "a total deviation from reality as most of us know it." As he gravitated from stone to stone, trying to make out the weathered carvings, he felt a persistent tapping on his shoulder, but each time he turned

112

around he saw no one. After ten minutes of this odd annoyance he felt something yank at the back of his coat collar,
nearly knocking him off his feet. He recovered and whirled
around, his heart beating double-time. No one was there.

At this point Dr. Rutger did what any of us would do—he
resolved to book it from the graveyard. But as he started toward the nearest exit, he noticed something out of the corner
of his eye: "I saw a young girl standing motionless in the rear
corner of the cemetery, staring at me intently." She wore a
white dress, and her utter immobility in and of itself seemed
eerie. Dr. Rutger turned in the opposite direction, but, to his
amazement, the girl instantly relocated to the front of the
cemetery, nearly fifty yards from where she'd stood only
moments before. Dr. Rutger changed direction a couple more
times, and each time the ghostly figure cropped up at a different station. Finally he made it to the sidewalk, but as he strode
away he felt a hand slip into his pocket. He watched in amazement as his car keys levitated free of his pocket, dangled in
mid-air, then fell with a jingle to the ground. After he retrieved
his keys, he crossed the street and stepped back into the real
world. Nothing else out of the ordinary occurred to him.

Later, however, the dentist reflected, "One thing is certain:
the encounter affected me in very profound ways. As a trained
medical professional, I have always seen the world in fairly
empirical terms. Now, after experiencing what I did, I realize I
don't have the footing I once had. There's no way something
like that cannot completely change how you think about
the world."

What few visitors to Boston realize is that all forty-eight
acres of Boston Common, the park founded in 1634, are actually one big anonymous burying ground, even apart from the
specifically designated Central Burying Ground. Under the
repressive Puritan regime, untold numbers of miscreants—
murderers, thieves (including one "highway robber" named

Rachell Whall, who, in the late 1700s, pinched a seventy-five-cent bonnet), pirates, Indians, deserters, Quakers, and putative witches—were executed on the Common.

The most famous so-called witch to die on this spot was Mary "Goody" Glover, an Irishwoman who spoke fluent Gaelic but little English, which alone sufficed to land her in trouble. At her trial her inability to quote the Lord's Prayer in English struck her accusers as proof positive she was the Devil's hand-maiden. Her actual crimes, which sociologists would identify centuries later, were that she was perfectly self-sufficient (she happened to be a widow) and she was outspoken and opin-ionated and therefore not particularly well liked: the precise profile of most women executed as witches in Colonial times. Glover's luck ran out when her daughter instigated a fight with a neighbor's daughter, and shortly thereafter the neigh-bor's kids were, according to court records, "horribly taken with fits," including mysterious pains, darting tongues, twisting heads, roaring—in short, the whole repertoire of demonic tics demonstrated so impressively by Linda Blair in *The Exorcist.* The community blamed Goody Glover for the group hysteria, and she was hanged from Boston Common's infamous Great Elm on November 16, 1688.

That tragic tree, on the Tremont Street side, blew down in a gale in 1876, but in fact most Boston hangings from 1769 on-ward took place on the northwest Charles Street section of the Common, now the site of a massive subterranean parking garage. In Colonial times part of the punishment of public ex-ecution was to leave the body dangling—and decomposing— indefinitely. At risk to their own lives, friends and family might sneak in under cover of darkness, cut down the cadaver, and bury it somewhere in the park. If no one came forward to deal with the disastrous remains, town officials eventually dis-posed of them in the river, where bloated bodies frequently washed in and out with the tides.

Given this sorrowful history, it's no wonder that an atmosphere of melancholy hangs over Boston Common. On the surface it appears an idyllic spot, a city version of a Grandma Moses watercolor, with skaters pirouetting on the iced-over Frog Pond in winter, and in summer, picnickers lounging beside the great granite fountain near Park Street. But pay attention, and you'll feel the psychic imprint of misfortune hanging over the rolling greensward. You'll notice that few flowers are planted here; unlike other parks in Boston, where blossoms abound, nothing festive can thrive for long in this energy vortex of unjust killings and unmarked graves. The Common's sister site is London's Green, where in the sixteenth century a mass grave was dug for victims of the Black Death. There municipal gardeners have given up trying to implant even the humblest petunias; they simply won't flourish. And office workers who take their lunches into Green Park feel after five or ten minutes an intangible sadness stealing over them, causing them to pack up their repast and retreat from the grounds.

It's not that Boston Common isn't one of the most wonderful parts of the city. You might crisscross its paths several times a day and love it, but it is perhaps ill-advised to linger there. If it's a longer stay, perhaps a picnic, you're after, you may find your jug of wine and loaf of bread more easily digested in another city park.

⊱ 15 ⊰

The Sentry at the Huntington Theatre

All old and beautiful theatres look haunted, with their shadowy corridors, flickering lanterns, vaulted ceilings, and Gothic ornaments. They also sound haunted, from the creaking of woodwork, the rustling of old pipes, the sighs of air currents trapped inside thick stone walls. And indeed, there are some who contend that all old and beautiful theatres really *are* haunted!

Here's why: Anyone who has spent time around actors knows they are most alive on stage and in the company of other show folk. The make-believe they create on the boards becomes reality, and what the rest of us call real life is spent biding time in a functional catatonia between performances. Therefore, when an actor dies and happens to rematerialize as a ghost, it will surely rush on ectoplasmic wings to its favorite playhouse. We could even take this argument a step further and allege that, for many deceased actors, a return to the stage exerts a stronger pull than the tunnel of light leading to heaven.

London's most famous theatrical ghost is the Man in Gray of the Theatre Royal in Drury Lane. For more than two hundred years, the immobile figure in a gray cloak and three-cornered hat, with a sword at his belt, has been spotted by dozens of people in his favorite stall in the upper circle. Rumors suggested that the figure had in life been obsessed with a beautiful actress, whom he watched from this height, but that he'd antagonized her husband and was slain in a duel. Stories of this melodramatic pitch are usually written off as exaggeration, if not outright fiction, but in 1850 a shocking discovery was made: A work crew hired to knock down the wall of the upper circle discovered a hidden chamber containing a skeleton with a dagger run through its ribs. An autopsy took place, an open verdict was declared, and the authorities buried the remains in consecrated ground around the corner from the theatre. Still, this respectful conclusion for the Man in Gray's remains hasn't prevented him from frequenting the upper circle; habits of theatregoers die hard.

America's most famous theatrical ghost is linked to the malevolent vortex left in the wake of the events of April 14, 1865, when actor and assassin John Wilkes Booth emptied his derringer into Abraham Lincoln's head at Ford's Theatre in Washington, D.C. In the pandemonium that broke out, Booth charged across the stage to escape, knocking down actors right and left. Later he was cornered in a barn and shot to death by an enraged militia.

For over a century the abandoned Ford's Theatre stood as a hulking ruin and a monument to one of our nation's great tragedies. Then, in 1968, the building was refurbished as a museum and working playhouse, and a strong occult presence has made itself known there ever since. Curtains rise and lower by themselves, lights go on and off without human supervision. Footsteps echo in empty halls, and disembodied voices, laughter, and sobs erupt from all sides of the house. Booth's personal stamp is sensed in the last deranged sprint he took across the stage. Actors wandering into this occult zone have felt suddenly nauseated. Others tremble uncontrollably. They forget their lines or, worse, blank out altogether, losing all memory of what play they're performing. Famous actors such as Hal Holbrook and Jack Aaronson have reported that as they crossed Booth's zigzag line of evil, they experienced a frightening drop in temperature.

Other noteworthy haunts include the Belasco Theatre in New York, where the ghost of founder David Belasco can be seen in his signature monk's outfit; and the Palace Theatre, also in New York, where a tightrope walker once plunged to his death, and where, to this day, a phantom fall and piercing scream are reenacted before the debut of any new production destined for failure (there isn't a Palace producer alive who cares to hear that The Ghost fell from his tightrope the night before). At the Old Met, also in New York, a Mrs. Frances Alda, ex-wife of long-ago director Gatti Cazzaza, used to show up in her front-row stall to harangue whichever soprano had the misfortune to be cast in the current production. The psychotic behavior was bad enough in life; imagine the chagrin of singers, Met officials, and audience members when an apparition of the deceased ex–Mrs. Cazzaza appeared from time to time to spoil the first act of a new opera. On one occasion a woman in a nearby seat complained to the head usher about the loudmouth in the front stall. The usher took the plaintiff aside, gave her a glass of sherry, and explained the situation with the ghost.

Thus, in a world of haunted theatres, to say that Theatre Y is more riddled with spooks than Theatre Z is like swearing that one barbecue smells more strongly of steak than a hundred others. All the same, in Boston it's well known in both theatrical and parapsychological circles that the Huntington Theatre, located at 264 Huntington Avenue, is one of the city's premier creep-out sites.

An actress named Carla once dropped off for a nap on a sofa in the Huntington's Green Room. She felt a hand jostle her awake—it was a friend, pointing out, with trembling arm, an apparition of a woman in white floating above the carpet. The women later learned that the Lady in White was a departed wardrobe mistress who flutters over dress rehearsals. Other actors have seen the ghost of the late Shakespearean actor Henry Jewett, perhaps best known for his role in *Macbeth*, the play most actors insist on calling by any other name (such as "The Scottish Play," "The Unmentionable," or "The Caledonian Tragedy") to avoid fallout from the dreadful curse said to attend productions of . . . "that play."

Carla reported that other actors at the Huntington have glimpsed a ghostly figure strolling on the catwalk, high above the stage. And in the millinery shop every afternoon around 3:15, the worker on duty observes a shadow flickering overhead, a sight that causes newcomers to gasp, "Who's there?!" A friend of Carla's, Denise, was in the hat storage room when she felt a hot hand on the back of her neck. She turned with a start but saw no one. Another time someone grabbed her hip, and again she found herself completely alone in the dimly lit storage room.

An actor/playwright named Daryl maintained that many players at the Huntington have seen a ghost they call The Sentry, a grainy black figure who stalks the hall outside the Green Room. Many have either seen him, heard his footsteps, or felt his presence, or all of the above. The popular belief is that The Sentry patrols the halls as a one-man security force, and after a person's nervous first exposure to him, he is accepted as a sign that all is safe and sound inside the theatre. Because of The Sentry's protective quality, he's generally taken to be the ghost of the Huntington's founder. According to legend, he built the grand 850-seat theatre as a shrine to his actress wife, who, midway through construction, cruelly abandoned him. When the theatre was completed, the founder chose that symbolic moment to commit suicide.

Stories as lurid as this one are often the make-believe with which kids scare each other over melted marshmallows and a roaring campfire. Indeed, nothing in the Huntington Theatre records suggests that a heartbroken impresario killed himself over his wife's betrayal. And it would seem that any actress worth her salt, or her ego's salt, would have waited to star in at least one production—perhaps as Lady Macbeth?—before lowering the boom on her lovelorn husband.

If the playhouse, which opened in 1925 as the Repertory Theatre of Boston, suffered from any sort of haunting at the outset, it had more to do with the economics of 1920s entertainment: Five years after ringing up its curtains, the theatre sat dark and abandoned, done in by the historic moment when Al Jolson opened his mouth to sing "Mammy," and large numbers of patrons deserted live theatre in favor of a newer form of amusement, the movies they called "the talkies."

A more plausible identity for The Sentry would be the indomitable Hallie Flanagan, who, from 1935 to 1939, restored life to the big theatre on Huntington Street through the Federal Theatre Project. Hallie stood not a millimeter over five feet, unless you measured the flamboyant hats she liked to wear. But the lady was possessed of what John Houseman called "visionary obstinacy." In the days when women were not only not expected to have it all, but to have *nothing* outside of the home, this one-woman locomotive created an arts relief project that transcended the genre and created a national theatre, at its height employing twelve thousand theatrical workers across the country. Early on, Hallie had lost her husband to tuberculosis and one of her two sons to spinal meningitis; this double tragedy fostered her lifelong habit of burying sorrow beneath a drive equal to six workhorses.

The Federal Theatre Project was Hallie's ultimate labor of love, and it broke her heart when, in 1939, the nascent House Committee on Un-American Activities pulled the plug on the project's budget. She did get back at the hateful congressmen, however: Called to testify, she was asked to explain her theatre troupe's being endowed with what she'd called in the press "a certain Marlowesque madness." Representative Joseph Starnes of Alabama wanted to know who was this dangerous left-winger, Marlowe? Hallie Flanagan replied haughtily, "Put it in the record that [Christopher Marlowe] was the greatest dramatist in the period immediately preceding Shakespeare."

Flanagan died in 1968, and if there's any spirit more likely to flit over the boards of the Huntington, it would be hard to imagine who that pillar of passion might be. Of course, there's plenty of room for a platoon of ghosts inside the immense stone walls of the theatre. And, judging by the testimony of the Huntington's cast and crew, a platoon it is, indeed.

⇒ 16 ⇒

America's Oldest Haunted Hotel

So many famous people have churned through the gilded halls of the Omni Parker House, in the heart of Old Boston, that one of them, Oliver Wendell Holmes, penned a tribute to the glitzy procession: "Such guests! What famous names its record boasts, whose owners wander in the mob of ghosts!"

Mr. Holmes may not have been referring to literal ghosts, but nowadays this grande dame of Boston hotels at the corner of Tremont and School Streets is known for genuine spirits in addition to the echoes left by departed guests of great renown. Literary lights such as Emerson, Thoreau, Hawthorne, and Longfellow formed The Saturday Club at the Parker House for the sharing of food, drink, wit, and tall stories. Charles Dickens resided there for months at a stretch, plying club members and other guests with his recipe for English gin punch (he requested a reinforced table in his suite to support the jumbo punch bowl). In those days, top authors received the attention of today's rock stars, and Mr. Dickens was sometimes forced to barricade himself in his rooms when throngs of fans clustered in the hall, hoping for a glimpse of him.

Theatre greats such as Sarah Bernhardt, Edwin Booth, and Edwin's infamous brother, John Wilkes (more about him momentarily) occupied the Parker House's luxurious suites. Later guests included Judy Garland, Joan Crawford, and Madonna. Baseball legends Babe Ruth and Ted Williams devoured the hotel's world-class cuisine. Through the years, the Parker has probably hosted more U.S. presidents than any other hotel in the country, from Ulysses S. Grant to FDR to JFK to Bill Clinton; and the staff has been a training ground for movers and shakers such as Malcolm X and Ho Chi Minh, who once bused tables at the restaurant.

From the beginning, however, the site of the Parker House reverberated with darker notes from American history. In 1704 a fine brick house stood on the spot, built by a wealthy French businessman for his wife, the former Miss Brattle (of Brattle Street, Cambridge). In 1770, a snowfall inspired boys from Boston Latin School to sled down the slope with whoops and hollers. Annoyed at these antics, the local British constabulary spread ashes over the snow. The boys retaliated by heaving rocks. One thing led to another, and a riot broke out. Redcoats fired on the crowd. The smell of gunpowder hung in the air as five young Bostonians lay dead on the frosty ground.

The psychic imprint of the horror known as the Boston Massacre may have caused what parapsychologists call an aura of disaster—fertile ground for the birthing of ghosts. Down through the ages, at the corner of Tremont and School Streets, one specific spook has captured the most attention, and this is none other than the hotel's founder, Harvey Parker.

The hotelier's saga is one of those rags-to-riches stories that bejewel the history of American capitalism. Born in 1805 on his father's farm in Temple, Maine, Harvey hopped a packet ship for Boston at the age of twenty-one. He had twenty-five cents in his pocket and a few articles of clothing stuffed in a scarf—the classic hobo gear. From his first humble job in a Watertown mill he graduated to coachman for a rich lady who dined weekly in town. While his employer ate oysters and pheasant in champagne sauce, Harvey enjoyed mutton and mashed potatoes in a pub around the corner. An opportunity to buy the pub arose, and Harvey, on the strength of his lifelong interest in fine cuisine, went for it, changing the name to Parker's.

If you cook it (well), they will come could have served as his motto, for it wasn't long before Parker's became one of the most popular restaurants in the city. From as far afield as Cambridge, Harvard students flocked to Parker's doors, leading one wit to dub it "The Harvard Annex." In 1855 Harvey Parker hired a chef from Paris for the staggering annual salary of five thousand dollars (most Boston cooks received eight dollars a week). The restaurant's culinary productions grew more lavish every season. A typical eleven-course meal consisted of oysters; green turtle soup; baked cod in claret sauce; partridge with truffles and jelly; mayonnaise of chicken; compote of pigeons; blue-billed widgeon; bird nest pudding; calf's-foot and madeira jellies; charlotte russe with mince, squash, lemon, or apple pie; and an abundance of oranges, peaches, walnuts, almonds, and raisins. (Was it any wonder the rich and fat of the era had to journey twice a year to health spas to work off acute symptoms of gout?)

A passion for good food combined with a genius for business: Parker's, the successful restaurant, led to the construction in 1854 of a magnificent European-style hotel. Parker went on expanding the premises until it resembled a French château, with an eight-story white marble facade. In keeping with the style of the times, the dormers, chimneys, ledges, and eaves were ornamented with every type of Victorian gewgaw, from marble griffins to gilded acanthus leaves, but the decoration that caused the biggest stir—and later led to speculation that it may have attracted occult activity—was the ring of thirteen wrought-iron black cats encrusting the ridge pole.

A little more than 105 years after the Boston Massacre, another sinister influence touched down on the property at Tremont and School. On April 5, 1865, John Wilkes Booth checked into the Parker House and dined at its world-class restaurant. He may have dropped in on a performance by his infinitely more talented brother, Edwin, at the three-thousand-seat Boston Theater; the younger sib's attendance remains uncertain. But one of John Wilkes Booth's activities was known and duly reported when its full significance later came to light. He paid a visit to a shooting gallery not far from the hotel, where he practiced fancy postures such as firing from between his legs and over his shoulder. On April 14, Booth departed Boston for Washington, D.C., and Ford's Theatre, where he assassinated President Abraham Lincoln.

Back in Boston, the Parker House staff were appalled to think of their recent guest reclining in one of their rooms as he plotted the crime of the century.

On May 31, 1884, Harvey Parker died at the age of 79. Well, ostensibly he died. The fact is, his spirit has materialized from time to time, continuing to cater to his clients' needs. Occasionally guests wake to find a proper nineteenth-century gentleman with a kindly, bearded face, perched at the ends of their beds. On their startled reaction he replies, "I've come to check on your accommodations. Do you have everything you require?" Other times Harvey Parker has been sighted wandering the tenth-floor corridors, a heavyset figure in a Victorian frock coat, looking solid at first glance, then gradually fading away.

It's worth noting that, while the ghostly hotelier's favorite haunt appears to be the tenth floor, that floor didn't exist during his reign, when the edifice stood no higher than eight stories. In 1927 the Whipple Corporation razed the old white marble palace and erected in its place a fourteen-story shrine to luxury, with a facade of polished Quincy granite. The new edifice housed eight hundred guest chambers, and the public rooms featured soaring ceilings, oak paneling, bronze-detailed ornamentation, and Waterford crystal chandeliers the size of small boats. It's pretty much the hotel we know today (subsequently renovated in the 1990s by the Omni chain).

It's not difficult to see how all these changes may have spun the head of Harvey's spirit. If he's prowling the tenth floor he must be wondering what it's doing there in the first place! Longtime staffer Ed Cotto has heard reports of large, nebulous white lights on the ninth and tenth floors, and on other occasions he says hotel workers have noted unexplainable thumps and grinding noises. Ed recalled: "One guy heard the sounds, and it upset him so much he had to go home for the day."

The third floor holds its own complement of occult symptoms. One of the three elevators with the ornate, bronze-leaf doors has been known to travel to the third floor without a single button being pressed. Nowadays this seldom occurs, but for years the left-hand elevator would take off by itself, chime its bell at level three, and trundle open its doors, whereupon no one would emerge. This ascent to the third floor happened hundreds of times. Engineers combed the system repeatedly without discovering the flaw.

It was on this third floor that Charles Dickens spent his madcap months at the Parker House, with writers, artists, celebrities, and zany Boston personalities milling through his rooms and downing gallons of his English gin punch. As previously mentioned, flocks of fans stalked the corridors, waiting to pounce on the most famous author of the age. Perhaps some sort of "muscle memory" in the elevator system recalls the excitement of those times and continues to disgorge phantoms of parties past to Dickens's door. (The actual door is gone, along with the older building, but a gigantic mirror hangs on the mezzanine—the mirror in front of which the author practiced reading *A Christmas Carol* before performing it for a live audience.)

Another historical tidbit lends an additional factor to the third-floor hauntings. For eighteen years the first lady of the American stage, Charlotte Cushman, revered for her ability to act both female and male parts with equal believability, lived in the Dickens suite of the Parker House. Lying in her hotel bed in 1876, Charlotte Cushman, age 60, drew her last breath. So perhaps the elevator rolls open its empty cabin for her as well? Or does it suppose she's late for the theatre?

One final spectral element afflicts the third floor. Some years ago a businessman died in Room 303. Ever since that time, the odor of whiskey infuses the room. Occasionally a small fire sparks in the wastebasket, and guests have heard rude male laughter with no actual rude male to back it up. Room 303 caused so many problems that the management eventually retired it as guest quarters, converting it to a storage closet. Of course, if whatever's stored in there begins to reek of whiskey or spontaneously combust, the management will again need to rethink the room's function.

Seamus Murphy, a twenty-five-year veteran of the hotel staff, said that several years ago a housekeeper was turning over a suite of rooms for an arriving VIP when she heard the shower running in what she knew to be an empty bathroom. When she went to investigate, she found the shower faucet turned off, but damp towels lay crumpled on the floor. Another time a security guard, patrolling the Bosworth wing at night, was startled by the sight of a shadow of a tall man in a Victorian stovepipe hat, projected on the wall. Seamus said that after that incident the security guard eliminated the Bosworth wing from his beat, drawing untold ribbing from staffers amused at the notion of a professional "rent-a-cop" being afraid of shadows.

Another longtime staff member, doorman Rich Aliferis, recalled a long-ago night when an airline pilot guest saw a shadowy figure slip into his closet. The pilot called security, and when the team arrived, they found the closet unaccountably locked. The man insisted that they take an ax to the doors. When they broke through, they found nothing inside other than two clean, white terry-cloth robes.

Whatever's happening at the Omni Parker House these days, it's safe to say it's all part of the ambiance of America's longest continuously operating hotel. With all those layers of history, all the tens of thousands of people who've lived, loved, partied, won acclaim, plotted assassinations, dropped face-first into Charles Dickens's punch bowl, and, yes, died there, you're bound to get a number of continuously operating ghosts.

PART V

Haunted Outer 'Hoods

The Samuel A. Way House, Parker Hill, Roxbury, 1890s
Photo by A. H. Folsom, BOSTON PUBLIC LIBRARY PRINTS DEPT.

Radiating out from
Boston's center are a slew of neighborhoods
with fully as much history, color, and charm
as any part of the inner city. Each neighborhood
has its own special character: Dorchester,
with its multi-ethnic neighborhoods and the oldest
house in greater Boston; Jamaica Plain,
with its trees and pond and bohemian élan;
South Boston, with its pubs, parades, and parish
churches. And ghosts. We'll examine a few
of the spectres from a few of the surrounding
neighborhoods to get some sense
of how the supernatural layers of Boston
spiral outward from the core.

⊸ 17 ⊸

House of Nightmares

D erek still has bad dreams about the house, even though six
years have elapsed since he escaped from it.

In July 1996, Derek and his friend Paul, both in their mid-
twenties, found a house in Everett, on the outskirts of Boston,
that seemed the perfect bachelor pad. The landlord, a Vietnam
vet who'd had his legs blown off below the knees in the war,
had renovated the three-bedroom house, adding a wheelchair
ramp, a satellite television disk, and play space for his kids. But
he never moved his family into these ideal quarters; instead, all
five of them led a cramped existence in a first-floor apartment
at the front of the property that had none of the comforts
of the rental house. Derek assumed his landlord needed the
rental income badly enough to forfeit the cottage.

The house did have one odd characteristic: it was cut off
from all surrounding streets. Tenants had to walk through the
landlord's or other neighbors' backyards to get to their quarters. Derek selected the back bedroom for himself, only to discover that he peered out on the drab brick wall of a mortuary.
"It was so close, I could stick my arm out the window and
practically touch it." In the confined space between the buildings was a tiny, neglected garden housing a statue of the

Virgin Mary covered with moss, and some sort of thorny bramble. "Our house seemed to overpower the statue," recalled Derek.

Their first night in the cottage, as Derek settled into bed, he found his gaze irresistibly and yet morbidly drawn to his closet, a plain wooden wardrobe. "I kept having these strange feelings that there was something inside staring straight through the door at me." He solved the problem the way little kids do: he pulled his covers over his head, burrowed deep down in the mattress, and willed himself to sleep. The next morning, over breakfast, he learned that Paul had passed an even stranger night in one of the other bedrooms. He was repeatedly awakened by an elderly female voice moaning, "It's not my fault."

The next week passed uneventfully, but then one day Derek started feeling as if he were under attack every time he entered his room. "I sensed there was someone inside the closet, watching me. All the time. It was unnerving."

One bright Saturday morning Derek and another friend, Joe, decided to explore the basement. They walked past a sheet of plastic that suddenly ruffled as if from a wind, though how that could happen below ground, with no open windows, was incomprehensible. They discovered that the plastic covered an original stone foundation in the middle of the basement floor. Derek and Joe peeled the tarp away to find themselves staring through a hole into a second, lower basement. They grabbed flashlights and lowered themselves into the hole. Tucked into a corner was a pile of white, powdery dust. Derek pushed the pile aside, feeling like Huck Finn about to stumble upon the skull of an ancient Indian. Instead he uncovered a heavy implement, about two-and-a-half feet long, with a hook at the end, pitted with rust. It looked like some sort of tool for stacking lumber.

Derek recounted, "We were total idiots, but we brought it upstairs, and that's when all hell broke loose."

That evening Derek and Paul sprawled on the couch, watching television. "What's that?" said Paul, jumping up. They froze at the sound of heavy footsteps stomping in the attic. All of a sudden, the racket overhead was forgotten as Paul shouted, *"Stand up, man! Stand up!"* Derek stood, and immediately he felt something slam the floor beneath his feet. "Like someone was downstairs, punching the ceiling!" Both young men stared dumbfounded as the soles of their feet absorbed the shocks.

"We spent the next two hours with our feet propped up, but we couldn't stop asking one another, 'What was that?!' "

A few nights later Derek climbed into bed with an intensified sense of someone observing him. He shut off the light, and all at once a figure shimmered at the end of the bed, seated on thin air. It was an old woman clad in a silken white gown imprinted with ivy leaves. Two ivy leaves covered her eyes.

"I felt waves of hatred pouring from her!" Horrified, he ran from the room and spent the night on the couch. "I never slept in my room again for the whole nine months that we lived in the house."

But he felt only nominally safer in the living room. One night he ventured into the forbidding precinct of his bedroom to fetch some books. As he returned to the dining room through the long hallway, he felt eyes boring into his back. Spinning around, he saw a nine- or ten-foot shadowy shape extending from floor to ceiling. It had texture, but it was also semi-transparent, as if he could walk through it, if he dared. "I felt every ounce of strength and energy leave me and get sucked into that thing. It was directing beams of hatred at me, and I knew it wanted me out of the house. I sensed that it had never been human. It had never known love, nor did it want to. It was a demon. Something very, very evil."

Derek screamed and fled into the living room, where he roused Joe from a TV-induced stupor. "Wha—?" sputtered Joe, "What happened?" Derek kept screaming and pointed to the hallway. Joe stood and with a manful stride went to investigate. A moment later he hurtled out, flinging himself back on the sofa.

"Did you see it?" asked Derek.

"No, but I could feel it," Joe said, sounding every bit as shaken as his friend.

The next months unraveled in a haze of scary images. Crashes and booms erupted in the rooms. Derek sometimes stood in the shower to see a shadow float past the frosted glass door. He endured recurrent dreams of his family members being brutally murdered. His weight dropped from 135 pounds to 110 pounds. "I looked like a walking skeleton. My mother thought I had leukemia or something." Perhaps the worst dimension of the haunting was the personality change effected in the two roommates, as well as their constantly visiting buddies: "Paul, a really mellow guy, turned into a complete control freak. My friend Neil, who was an introvert, started to act like a spoiled brat. Joe used to be as honest as a Boy Scout, but suddenly he was conniving and stealing stuff! And as for me, before I moved into the house I was going to conquer the world and make my first million before I turned thirty. After I'd been in the house for a while, I morphed into a total slug, lost my job, and made no plans to get a new one."

Before forfeiting his job, however, Derek made the acquaintance of a coworker named Tony, who moonlighted as a voodoo *houhgan*. After getting to know him on the job, Derek became convinced of Tony's psychic abilities and, without providing any of the details, invited Tony to his house to see whether he might pick up some of the bad vibes. The minute Tony entered the house, he pronounced it a supremely unhealthy atmosphere. He walked into Derek's bedroom and said with a sigh, "Oh boy, this is really bad." He approached the closet and, after wedging himself inside, instructed Derek to close the doors behind him. Less than a minute later, Tony flung the closet doors wide and propelled himself out. He stalked to the living room and sat down on the couch to catch his breath. At last he told Derek, "A little boy went insane in your room. This happened a long time ago. He lived here with his grandmother, and afterward she was blamed for his condition. There is so much sorrow inside these walls!"

Derek asked him about the demonic presence he'd encountered in the hallway. Tony prowled the entire house, from the foundation within the basement to the attic, where footsteps and other assorted noises had erupted. Finally he explained that the demon had been lured here by the intense suffering of the original family members. Now it was trapped inside the premises. "He spins and spins and spins, and the more he spins, the more he laughs, and the more he laughs, the more he gets off on his own laughter. Once he builds up enough energy, he manifests a load of paranormal activity in the house."

Derek asked Tony if he could exorcise the demon and the ghosts of the grandmother and grandson from the property. The voodoo priest shook his head. "The house perverts everyone who walks into it. It would be safer for you to just leave it to its own tragic fate."

He advised Derek to move out.

"You sound like my mother," said Derek.

At last Derek and Paul decided to board with their parents while they scrimped and saved to start again in a new rental. For a long time, however, Derek found his thoughts revolving obsessively around the house he'd abandoned. "I used to park across the street and stare past the landlord's yard to the front door. The place stayed empty for about two months, then a couple with a small boy moved into it. I felt awful for them. But after a month they moved out. No surprise there!"

The last tenancy occurred in March 1997, and the house remained deserted as of Derek's reporting in the fall of 2001. "On a scale of one to ten," he said, "Ten being the Amityville Horror house, I would have to give this place an eight."

Both asleep and awake, he still suffers recurring night-mares about the property. "I can't get this image out of my mind of the mortuary statue of the Virgin Mary, covered in thorns, more and more of them as the seasons go by ... "

⇒ 18 ⇒

Better than Embalming

In the mid-nineteenth century, the pleasant suburb of Malden, just north of Boston, had one unpleasant citizen: Ephraim Gray lived alone in a big weathered house near the heart of town. He had no wife, no relatives, and no friends, and any attempt to engage him in neighborly chitchat was met with a grunt and a cold shoulder. Only a man of means can afford the lifestyle of so cranky a recluse, holed up alone in his house without discernible profession, so it was assumed Ephraim Gray had private means. His sole concession to human contact was a purely pragmatic one: he employed a manservant to cook, clean, and run all the errands requiring contact with the outside world.

When an old lady lives alone in a spooky house, she's assumed to be a witch. If the shut-in is male, he soon materializes in the community's imagination as a Man of Mystery. So it was with Ephraim Gray. It was the rare Malden villager, strolling past the house on a dark night, who could resist taking a peek at the man's silhouette in an upstairs window. What was the old curmudgeon doing in the dimly lit room as he sat so still, virtually immobile? Worse was the terrible odor that sometimes oozed from the dwelling late in the afternoon—a chemical smell, of indefinable origin, that made passersby gag.

As the years went by and the villagers' lives changed, the only person whose situation stayed the same was Ephraim, with his immutable air of mystery. The house still guarded its dark secrets, and the unidentifiable stench continued to leak through the open windows. Then, one day in 1850, Mr. Gray's servant padded into the Malden police station to report that his employer had died.

It was following Ephraim's demise that the public finally learned what he had been up to all those years.

It surprised no one that the recluse had left nothing in his will to the town or any charities. His sole heir was his servant, and this loyal soul could retain his small fortune only if he carried out the following commandment: Between the time that Ephraim's body was removed from his house and the moment it was placed in a crypt at the local cemetery, nothing could be done to it. There must be no autopsy, no extraction of fluids, no embalming, no cutting or invasive procedure of any kind. The local mortician was appalled. Surely Mr. Gray would have desired certain select treatments to preserve his remains? In reply, the servant told an astonishing story:

His employer had been an amateur chemist who'd devoted years of research to a special formula that, once perfected, would ensure eternal youth and everlasting life. Unhappily, the mad scientist had fallen short of his goal. He'd tinkered with his elixir for years, but some final formulation eluded him. Before he died, however, he was convinced that the regular dosings he'd prescribed for himself over the years would keep his corpse daisy fresh. The funeral director gave in with a shrug; if a customer wished to arrive at his doorstep pre-embalmed, so much the better!

Ephraim Gray went to his final rest (or so it was believed) in the Malden Cemetery; his servant died a few years later. But the story about the crazy chemist and his after-death product lived on as Malden legend.

Twenty years elapsed. In a tavern in Cambridge one night, a group of Harvard medical students were unwinding over steins of beer. Perhaps they'd sat in on an autopsy that day or something in their studies elicited the subject, because one of the students, a fellow who happened to hail from Malden, related the story he'd heard in his youth about Mr. Ephraim Gray and his wild experiment. Suddenly the group was fired up to investigate—in the interest of science, of course! Whether they acted that very night or a few nights later is uncertain, but shortly after hearing about the Malden Man of Mystery, the students piled into a hired carriage to travel from Cambridge to the northern suburb. Sometime past midnight, they made their way to the cemetery and slipped inside. The Malden student led them to the dark crypt, and they heaved aside the mossy stone door.

With hammer and chisel, they carefully pried away the coffin's seal, then opened the lid. One of the students raised a lantern over the coffin. The others stared in shock. Ephraim Gray looked as if he'd been merely sleeping all those years. While his clothes showed the wear-and-tear of time, his flesh was smooth and rosy-hued, his hair lustrous and thick; in short, there was not a speck of decay to mark his two decades of shelf life in the crypt.

Carefully they closed the lid and resealed the coffin. They would need to keep the details of their excursion a strict secret: In earlier times Boston med students had been implicated in a rash of grave robberies, and now the penalties for such activities were harsh. If ever the Harvard men's prank came to light, they could kiss their medical careers goodbye.

The Malden youth tried to find out what had become of Ephraim Gray's formula. Apparently the obsessed chemist had left no notes that would allow his servant or anyone else to capitalize on his invention. Instead he'd taken it, and one last preservative dose, to his grave.

But Ephraim Gray's body had one more date with destiny.

In the early 1900s the highway department decided to run a new road through the part of Malden that included the cemetery. The plan entailed the excavation and reinterment of every burial. The relocation at first went smoothly, but workers hit a snag when they reached the Gray mausoleum. They had no problem dismantling the concrete cornice and walls, but they were brought up short to find the coffin suspiciously light. They opened the seals and pried up the lid, only to discover that the coffin was empty!

Almost as soon as the workmen stopped standing around scratching their heads, the authorities launched a thorough investigation. The story of the Harvard students' adventure in the crypt came to light, yet that only aggravated the mystery, for the coffin had in fact been perfectly resealed. The likely story was that one or more of the students had taken their dark endeavor further and returned to steal the body. But investigators believed the students—now in advanced middle age and ensconced in successful medical practices—when they swore they'd left the immaculate corpse in its tomb.

What other explanation can be gleaned from this tale? Certainly another grave robber could have appropriated the body for the autopsy market, but we also need to consider the unsettling notion that the chemist's formula had proved a keeper after all; that some two decades or more after his death and hibernation, Mr. Ephraim Gray had awakened, prised open his coffin lid, and strolled out into the night.

He might be living next door to any one of us. He might *be* any one of us! If you're out there, Mr. Gray, please contact a reputable psychic research society immediately!

⧧ 19 ⧧

The Ghost Who Lived in a Trailer

In the early 1960s, when the Boston Strangler stalked the city's streets, no one—especially women living alone—went to bed without first fastening every last lock, bolt, and latch on every last window and door. This was true of a gorgeous young stripper with the stage name of Rita Atlanta, recently widowed, who lived with her three kids and a pet skunk in a trailer on the outskirts of Boston. Born in Vienna before World War II, Rita had already imbibed her share of sorrows, and she'd learned to be on her guard after the Nazi occupation of her city forced her family to flee to America.

Rita had latent mediumistic abilities as well. One day back in Vienna, when she was eight years old and occupied with a box of crayons, something possessed her to put aside her childish scribblings of rainbows and puppies, and she filled an entire sheet with a highly detailed scene of a funeral. Seated at her side, her father was disturbed by so morbid a subject and asked her to explain. The little girl pointed out the mourners: this was her dad; these were various aunts, uncles, and siblings. And where was her mother? the man asked with a tense expression on his face. Rita pointed to the coffin.

Three weeks later her mother was dead.

Many years later, on a cold November night in the trailer park, Rita checked and double-checked her windows and doors. She made sure her kids were snug in their beds, then retired to her own tiny room. Her pet skunk for some reason lumbered out of her room and disappeared for the rest of the night. Sometime between three o'clock and three-thirty in the morning, Rita shook herself awake. She felt an overpowering presence close by. Thoughts of the Boston Strangler forced a scream to her throat. She opened her eyes to see a huge figure crowding her doorway. It was a man, almost seven feet tall, and weighing close to 350 pounds. He wore a long duster, and his face was obscured by both the darkness and the brim of a dark fedora. In a panic, Rita switched on the lamp beside the bed. Under the glare of the light the apparition evaporated, though Rita had a distinct impression he was still there, glowering at her.

For months the ghost put in regular appearances, subjecting Rita to three or four visits a week. Usually he hulked in the doorway. Other times he sat, feet dangling, on the kitchen counter, which was no more than a slab of vinyl-coated wood that would undoubtedly break under the heft of an actual flesh-and-blood man—especially a galoot like this one! Rita responded to the threat by sleeping with her bedroom lights ablaze. Concern about the electric bill finally compelled her to leave the lights off again, but that experiment lasted less than one night. Once again, she jerked awake past three in the morning to behold the big man in the dark coat and fedora massed in her doorway. The lights stayed on for another few weeks.

The ghost showed every sign of clinging permanently to the trailer. Rita, however, periodically removed herself when she took off for nightclub gigs in Europe, stashing her kids with friends. It was during one of these tours in Stuttgart,

Germany, that she decided to write to famous ghost hunter Hans Holzer. Mr. Holzer was intrigued by the woman's story as well as her background. He learned she'd been married to an air force pilot who'd encouraged his wife to shift from ballet to belly dancing and eventually to exotic dancing. On the ghost hunter's subsequent trip overseas, he and his wife, Catherine, dropped in at the German cabaret where Rita performed in a gargantuan champagne glass filled with "bubbly." The next morning, the stripper visited the Holzers at their hotel and filled them in on her occult traumas back home in the trailer park.

Mr. Holzer asked whether the ghost appeared to be searching for something, and Rita said no. Did he ever take off his fedora? Not once. She explained, too, that there was never a sound—no clearing of a throat or footsteps or creaking floorboards. When the ghost hunter learned about Rita's early childhood experience of predicting her mother's death, he realized she had psychic abilities. Holzer was of the opinion that, while everyone can hear ghosts' thumps and bumps and observe their handiwork such as windows opening and closing by themselves, only mediums can actually *see* spirits. That might explain why this particular entity had attached itself to the clairvoyant stripper.

As soon as Rita and Mr. Holzer returned to the States, the ghost specialist paid a visit to the trailer. A cold, steady drizzle cast somber shadows over the interior of the shabby dwelling. Mr. Holzer took photographs of the areas Rita identified as the apparition's favorite spots. Later, in the darkroom, some of these pictures revealed unusual mirrorlike surfaces. The ghost hunter asked Rita's oldest son to perform some investigative work in the neighborhood. The boy learned that a few years earlier on the periphery of the trailer park, a man had been struck and killed by a car. Mr. Holzer speculated that perhaps the dead man, disoriented by the accident, had missed the usual pathway to the Other Side and instead lurched into Rita's trailer, drawn by her psychical energies.

Happily, the ghost hunter's fact-finding put an end to the ghost's visits. Rita Atlanta was able once again to sleep with the lights off. Mr. Holzer thought perhaps his lengthy discussion with Rita within the ghost's hearing might have jogged it into thinking the afterlife could more profitably be spent somewhere other than a trailer park in the Boston boonies. Hans Holzer never again heard from Rita, although he occasionally glimpsed in the local papers ads for "The Girl in the Champagne Glass." He thought it ironic that the dancer was more comfortable with the ogling eyes of hundreds of firemen in a Stuttgart dive than with the penetrating stare of one lost and lonely soul in a trailer park. Yet, if it were put to a show of hands, perhaps most of us would choose the Stuttgart firemen.

⊰ 20 ⊱

L'eau de Death

In September 2001, Tami Viera moved into a two-bedroom apartment on a quiet lane in Somerville, the working-class alternative to the tonier neighborhood of next-door Cambridge. "It was one of those prewar clapboard buildings, three stories, with an apartment on each floor. The owners and their two kids had the ground-floor apartment, and an artist rented the top for her studio, so I moved into the middle unit and decided to look for a roommate at my leisure."

Tami had just received her master's degree in physical therapy from a college in upstate New York. She was busy interviewing at various Boston hospitals, but another side of her entertained fantasies of a radical change: "I had this craving to work in a gallery and take classes in ceramics, and maybe become a part-time yoga instructor." She had a small inheritance to see her through this period of searching. In the meantime she spent the early fall days fixing up the apartment. The kitchen cabinets needed painting, and the front bedroom, which she'd claimed as her own, underwent a makeover to pale yellow walls with blue trim. She picked up an antique sleigh bed from an estate sale in Lexington, and, except for her laptop computer and printer on the cherry-wood desk, the room reminded Tami of a place Louisa May Alcott might have inhabited.

Imagine her surprise, then, when she came home one afternoon, crossed the threshold of her bedroom, and found the room reeking. "I thought a mouse had died in a vent or something." She searched diligently but could find no source for the odor. "A couple of times I gagged and had to run out of the room to clear my lungs."

No other nook or cranny of the apartment bore any trace of the smell. She dashed across the street to the corner store to load up on antibacterial cleansers to use on her bedroom walls and floor. "I pictured myself swabbing away for hours until the stink was gone."

When she returned with her supplies, she rolled up her sleeves and snapped on latex gloves. But when she entered her room, she found that the odor had lifted. Completely gone. "I didn't see how so strong a stench could vanish in ten minutes. Still, I was ecstatic that I didn't have to deal with it after all."

In October Tami found a roommate, Annie, a thirty-two-year-old psychologist who worked at a mental health clinic in Medford. A week after Annie moved in, she met Tami at the front door with a strained expression on her face. "Don't take this amiss, but your bedroom has this totally gross smell!"

With a sense of dread, Tami entered her room to confront the same odor that weeks earlier had sent her scurrying for cleaning products. This time she suggested that she and Annie take a walk around the block. Mystified, Annie nonetheless fell in with the plan. When they returned to the apartment a quarter-hour later, Tami made a beeline for her room with Annie on her heels. The stench was gone. But a couple of minutes later, Annie gave a squeal from her own room. Tami rushed in, prepared for the same smell to greet her there. Instead, the fragrance of rose petals washed over her, as if she'd burst upon a summer garden.

Tami's first thought was that it wasn't fair—why should her room get the stinkbomb and Annie's the bouquet of roses? But in the next moment she realized she wouldn't want to alienate her new roommate by having both their rooms reek!

Annie gave her a penetrating stare. "Is there a ghost in this apartment?"

"I don't know," answered Tami in all honesty. She'd had no experience with the paranormal, but she certainly doubted it would manifest as an odorama. Still, she was starting to open her mind to the possibility.

Two days later, Porter, Tami's boyfriend from Syracuse, came down to spend the weekend He'd never been to Boston, so she took him on the Freedom Trail and over to Charlestown to view the USS *Constitution*. They had dinner at a little trattoria in the North End. Later that night, as they started to drift off to sleep, Porter said, "What's that humming noise?"

Tami recognized it instantly. On quiet nights the muted drone of her printer could be heard from clear across the room. She climbed out of bed and nipped over to unplug the surge protector from the wall so that nothing electronic could disturb their night's rest.

A couple of hours later Tami and Porter were jostled from sleep by the sound of a clacking printer. Porter thrashed from under the blanket, and Tami sat upright. Her printer, though paperless, was rattling away as if she'd programmed it to spew out the first chapter of *War and Peace*.

"I thought you unplugged it!" cried Porter.

"I did!"

The printer continued to click and stutter, Tami turned on the light. Both she and Porter lurched over to her desk. She snatched the disconnected plug from the floor and held it up for her boyfriend's inspection. Gingerly they peered behind the desk, even as the printer went on madly scripting its paper-free epic. The wall socket was empty; Tami had connected all the desk appliances—computer, printer, lamp—to the surge protector sitting idle on the floor.

Porter whispered, "Quick! Put some paper in so we can see what the printer's communicating to us!"

"I'm out of paper."

"Borrow some from Annie."

"She's fast asleep!"

"Wake her up. This is important!"

"She just moved in! I don't want her to think I'm out of my mind!"

At that precise moment, the printer fell silent. Tami put her hands to her face and stared through her fingers from the printer to her boyfriend.

On Sunday, when Porter headed back to Syracuse, Tami descended the stairs and knocked on her landlords' door. The wife answered, a cute, plump woman who measured no more than five feet in height. A baby perched on her hip; a toddler peered out from behind her legs. Both kids had their mom's moon-shaped face and round green eyes.

Tami asked whether the woman knew about the strange goings-on in her apartment.

"Such as what?" asked the landlady.

Tami told her about the foul smell, the fragrance of roses, and the occult workings of her printer. The little woman nodded thoughtfully, inviting her inside. Over cups of tea at the kitchen table she told her that they'd encountered problems in the past, but that the last person to live there had called in a psychic exorcist and had assured them the apartment had been cleansed of all restless spirits.

"So why did this tenant leave?"

"She told us her company had transferred her. Why? Do you think—?"

The two women gazed at one another in silent speculation. Tami asked her landlady whether she had any idea of the source of the disturbances. The landlady helped her toddler lay out jacks on the tabletop, at the same time bouncing the baby on her knee as she explained, "My mother-in-law lived upstairs for the last two years of her life. She wasn't very happy about the situation. Even though we had round-the-clock care for her, and both Steven and I visited for hours every day, she still thought we'd shoved her out on the proverbial iceberg."

"Did she die..." Tami had difficulty completing the question, "in the apartment?"

The woman nodded.

"Which room?"

"The front bedroom."

Tami made a clean breast of the situation to her new roommate, telling her about the berserk printer and the information gleaned from their landlady. She was glad she'd confided in Annie, because now the two of them could compare notes and approach the puzzle together. They noticed that the bulletin board in the kitchen kept ending up face-down on the floor, even though the wall hook remained firmly in place. Annie tried propping it up on the breakfast nook table, ensconced behind several thick books and a decorative and very heavy antique iron. The next morning the bulletin board lay face-down again.

The dual smells continued, sometimes only the hideous smell in Tami's room, sometimes only the sweet floral scent in Annie's, sometimes both simultaneously or in rapid succession. The printer never again spewed out its mysterious *oeuvre*—a shame, as far as Tami was concerned, as after that first occasion she was careful to keep the machine filled with paper. "It would have been nice," she said wistfully, "for the ghost to give us a full accounting in plain English."

Annie pointed out that the spirit world might communicate through hieroglyphics, just as computers sometimes do when a glitch gets thrown into the system. The roommates would feel just as stymied staring at a piece of paper with incomprehensible signs on it. Tami agreed with her.

Meanwhile, real life intruded on the roommates' Somerville days. Annie's clinic began sharing her with two other units in Lowell and Salem, and the extra travel kept her away from home longer. Porter begged Tami to move back to Syracuse, but, although she missed him, she knew with a deep inner conviction that she was too young to settle down. As if to cement her decision, she accepted a job at Massachusetts General Hospital. Come spring, both roommates had learned to take the haunting in stride. The errant bulletin board was consigned to a closet, and they learned to patiently wait out the bad smell as it never lasted longer than ten minutes. Occasionally an item would go missing, but they learned not to tear up the apartment looking for it because it invariably turned up in its original setting hours later. Tami said, "It sometimes felt as if we lived in a controlled laboratory where some hidden technician with a clipboard would arrange everything each day. Sometimes the technician would forget to replace one of the articles, and as soon as he heard us squawking, he'd make a note to put it back ASAP."

By then Annie and Tami, both enjoying good salaries, decided to look for an apartment in the heart of town. "We found a fifth-story condo on Beacon Street in the Back Bay area," said Tami, "and there was no looking back. Although we stopped being frightened of whatever haunted the Somerville building, it was nice not to have your room smell like roadkill!"

So, who lives there now?

Tami professed ignorance on the subject. "All I know is that the place should have a regular exorcism, just the way other apartments need to be spring-cleaned and sprayed for bugs."

⇥ 21 ⇤

Engaged to a Ghost

A neat little aphorism about Dorchester is that, were it not a part of Boston, it could stand up as a vital little city in its own right. First off, it has its own righteous blend of Colonial history: In 1630 the Puritans landed at Mattapannock, now known as Columbia Point (site of the John Fitzgerald Kennedy Library and Museum). The newcomers cast about for a high, dry salient to protect themselves from Indians and built a fort on nearby Savin Hill. To stay truly grounded, in 1633 the settlers established the Dorchester North Burying Ground at Upham's Corner. The oldest surviving residence in Boston, Blake House, built in 1648, stands on Columbia Road between Boston and Dorchester Streets (the latter known locally as Dot Street). The Mather School on Meeting House Hill, originally a one-room schoolhouse, is the oldest elementary school in America.

During the Siege of Boston in 1776, George Washington and his ragtag band of patriots set up cannons on Dorchester Heights, routing the British under a continuous barrage of fire. In the first half of the 1800s the Dorchester wilderness gave way to rolling farmland, and this eventually ceded place to elaborate country homes for rich folk from the city several miles to the northwest. Commercial villages sprang up along the Neponset River and the harborfront, in turn attracting a trolley line inaugurated in 1857. To complete the march of progress, Dorchester was annexed in 1869 by Boston. From that time forward, Victorian manors have bejeweled the area, but the style of architecture distinctive to Dorchester is the three-family house nicknamed the "three-decker," popularized in the early 1900s.

It was in a Dorchester one-decker—i.e., a single-family dwelling—that our story takes place. In the 1950s Geoghan Killarney, age sixteen, was the oldest of nine brothers and sisters. His father owned a dry goods store, and in the late 1930s, with the Depression in full force, his dad bought for a song a six-bedroom Victorian, a little rundown but ideal for a large family, in a predominantly Irish neighborhood near Independence Square. "It was a great place for a kid to grow up," said Geoghan. "It was like everyone in town was your mother. The lady at the soda fountain would ask about your arithmetic test, the man at the corner grocery would let you take an apple for nothing, the nun sweeping the steps of the parish church would reach into her pocket for a hanky and wipe off your face if you were grimy from the baseball field."

It wasn't until Geoghan's sixteenth summer that he learned how, even in the most protective of communities, a threat can sometimes materialize out of thin air. On a sweltering August night, not a single breeze from the nearby sea wafted in to relieve the record high temperatures. Geoghan, on the threshold of adulthood, had been granted the only privacy possible in a house with nine siblings: he was given the attic for his bedroom. This worked fine most of the time, but on this hot and humid night he tossed and turned on his narrow bed, finally admitting that sleep was impossible in what was starting to feel like the upper pot of a double boiler. With a sigh, he heaved himself from bed and trekked three flights down to the front parlor, hoping to catch a breeze through the open bay windows facing the street.

A faint amber illumination stole in from the streetlight halfway down the block, glowing on the massive slabs of ornate Victorian furniture. Relieved to find himself in a cooler room, Geoghan sank down exhausted on an aged settee covered with worn chintz. He closed his eyes, wondering whether he could possibly sleep in an upright position.

All at once he was aware of someone perched beside him. He opened his eyes to see a young woman fixing him with a dark-eyed stare. She wore a white gown with a quantity of lace at throat and wrists. Her pale hair was pulled back in a topknot from which cascaded a veil of white tulle stitched with tiny pearls.

His first shock was succeeded by a second as he heard a rustling noise in front of him. He jerked up his head to see a man frowning down on him. The man looked to be about fifty years of age, and he wore what the astonished sixteen-year-old could only think of as museum duds—a black satin Victorian frock coat, a cream satin cravat, and a top hat. The man swept the hat from his head, tucked it under his right arm, and, juggling awkwardly, extracted a leather-bound Bible from a pocket deep inside his jacket.

Glaring at Geoghan, he declared in a gravelly voice, "You will marry my daughter." The apparition opened the book and read, "'Dearly beloved, we are gathered here today....'"

Geoghan's alarm hit the panic point, and he leapt from the settee to tear into the kitchen. His single abiding thought was that he must be dreaming. He switched on the cold water tap, bent his face over the sink, and splashed his flushed brow with water. In another moment, he hoped, he would wake up in his attic bedroom.

But on the contrary, as he lifted his dripping face, the silent bride appeared on his left. The next instant, the father/

reverend appeared on his right. Once again the stern figure opened his Bible. "'Dearly beloved,'" he intoned.

Geoghan bolted from the kitchen and fled up the three flights of stairs. When he reached his attic chamber, he locked the door and shoved a dresser in front of it. He threw himself on his bed, drawing the covers over his head. "I was still young enough to believe that if my head was hidden, I was safe." After five minutes of quaking under the scratchy fabric, he pulled the covers down just below his eyes. He braced himself to see the matrimonial duo standing at his bedside, but, to his infinite relief, he found himself alone in his room. "One really good thing about the ordeal was that I didn't even notice the heat anymore."

During his last year under his parents' roof, Geoghan never again experienced even a whisper of a ghostly event. Nor did he choose to speak to any member of his family about the phantom wedding. "I was afraid they'd pack me off to the loony bin!" But some fifteen years later, he and one of his now-grown sisters, Ruthie, met for dinner at a Boston tavern, and after a while the conversation steered itself toward childhood ghosts. It seemed both of them had been spooked in their family home: Geoghan by the enforced wedding, his sister by an elderly lady dressed in gray with a paisley scarf over her head who used to wake her early in the morning by tickling her feet. Oddly, Ruthie never found this frightening, although she, like Geoghan, thought it prudent never to mention it.

The occult visitor did provide Ruthie with an incentive to learn more about their house's history. Over the years she picked up tidbits about the property's past. The house had been built in the 1870s by a Dorchester whaling captain. Of his five children, four married, while the fifth, a girl, was jilted at the altar. The betrayal had made her reclusive or, in today's terms, agoraphobic. In her middle age, her mother died, and the daughter kept house for her father until he passed away a few years later. By the early 1900s all the houses in the neighborhood were outfitted with electricity—all but the home of the whaling captain's daughter. The elderly hermit was both penny-pinching and frightened of change, and eschewed all things electrical in favor of old-fashioned candles and gaslight. In her last years, her neighbors frequently glimpsed a single shimmer of light in the woman's otherwise pitch-black house, roving from window to window and up the stairs, as the solitary occupant carried her vestal flame. Shades of Miss Haversham in Charles Dickens's *Great Expectations*!

Dorchester's streets have harbored many cultures in addition to the Colonial, the Victorian, and later, the Irish. Now Hispanic and Cape Verdean families live adjacent to South Asian grocers and West Indian cafés that fill the sidewalks with scents of curry and other evocative spices. The grand summer homes survive for the most part, but they've been divided into apartments and crowded by other boarding houses as over the years the middle classes have left the area for the alleged paradise of suburban tract homes and shopping malls. Slowly Dorchester is being rejuvenated as more and more Americans find themselves longing for real community, where goods and services are within walking distance and where, to quote a recently popular television theme song, "everybody knows your name."

So, one of these days, if it hasn't happened already, a certain Victorian house near Independence Square could be purchased by people with pockets deep enough to restore it to a single-family dwelling. And then if certain conditions prevail—a hot and steamy August night, a young man alone in the downstairs parlor—the long-dead bride-to-be might don her white veil once more.

PART VI

Haunted Environs

✦ ✦

Old Witch House, Salem, corner of Essex and North Streets, 1862

Each of the picturesque
New England towns radiating out from
Boston has its share of ghost stories.
Concord, for example, is home to a Colonial-era
inn with a haunted honeymoon suite.
Provincetown harbors a severely haunted
sea captain's house, which is saying a lot in
a village simply loaded with haunted
sea captains' houses. Rehoboth, Gloucester,
Beverly—catch them at the right time, and they
all shimmer with an otherworldly veneer.
In the following stories we'll take a look
at a few of the spookier locales outside Boston,
leading up to the granddaddy (or perhaps
we should say the grandmommy)
of them all: Salem, Massachusetts. ⇥

⊨ 22 ⊨

The Village of the Lost Witches

Perhaps no one was ever meant to live on this lonely moor not far from the sea. Cape Ann, just northeast of Boston, is a jagged spit of land thrust out over the Atlantic like a finger testing for the first onslaught of a hurricane. A couple of miles inland, a barren plateau, bumpy with glacial boulders, conferred a sense of safety to the original settlers. These were farmers of early Colonial times, eager to stash themselves away from privateers, pirates, and other coastal predators.

In the nineteenth century, author Thomas Wentworth Higginson described a visit to the spot: "[We] found the hearthstones of a vanished settlement... an elevated tableland overspread with great boulders as big as houses and encircled with a girdle of green woods and another girdle of blue sea. I know nothing like that gray waste of boulders. ... In that multitude of monsters there seems a sense of suspended life; you feel as if they must speak and answer to each other—the silent nights, but by day only the wandering seabirds seek them, on their way across the Cape, and the sweetbay and green fern imbed there in a softer and deeper setting as the years go by."

This remote location can be accessed from either Rockport or Gloucester by following thorny paths until at last you reach the heath once known as Dogtown Common, original population one hundred, give or take a few. At first glance, you might think this isolated place, with brisk winds ruffling the tall grasses, is as primordial as the Serengeti Plain, untouched by human history. But if you meander around the boulders and peer closely at the ground, you'll come upon a cellar guarded by a time-pocked granite step. And what's that under the mass of blueberry bushes? Could it be the remains of a stone wall?

The Common's community dwindled after the Revolution, when British privateers were swept clear of the seaboard. With their safety thus ensured, at least theoretically, families packed up and moved to larger townships, particularly Gloucester, where fishing and shipping opportunities abounded. And when a road was carved along the shoreline from Gloucester to Rockport, a neglected village such as the Common, hard to reach and lashed by harsh winds, lost all reason for being.

A few of the original inhabitants, primarily widows loath to leave their cherished homes, stayed on. They kept large dogs to protect them, and when the widows died, the dogs ran wild, hence the name Dogtown.

Gradually a new breed of Dogtowner straggled in to Cape Ann. These *arrivistes,* hunkered down in abandoned houses, were the flotsam and jetsam of early eighteenth-century society—toothless old crones, homeless drunkards, and the occasional poor "lunatic" who'd escaped the dragnet of insane asylums. They subsisted on blueberries and whatever fish or fowl they could extort from traveling merchants. Extortion, in fact, was a specialty of the old crones, many of whom were notorious for their "vile langwich" and their ability to cast hexes.

An element of comic opera, or even situation comedy, pervaded the society of post-Revolutionary Dogtown. One of the so-called witches was Easter Carter, an Englishwoman respected for her healing arts and fortune telling. As chatelaine of the sole two-story house in the village, she set herself above the others. "I eats no trash," she maintained, in sneering reference to the scavengers who subsisted on blueberries and squirrel meat. She boarded two odd individuals, a wizardly Mr. John Woodman, and a freed slave named Old Ruth, who dressed in men's clothes and hired herself out as a day laborer, chopping wood and carting stones. Nearby neighbors of this winsome trio were broomstick rider (or so the rumors maintained) Peg Wesson and Aunt Becky Rich, who sold a feel-good tonic called Dire Drink, brewed from foxberry leaves, spruce tips, and Becky's secret herbs. When a villager succumbed to a cold, flu, or vapors, Aunt Becky sailed through the patient's door, crying, "Here, ducky, this'll make you feel springish!" Ever generous, the Dire Drink lady treated her fortune-telling customers to meals of boiled cabbage and cornbread—quite a good deal all around.

Other eccentric citizens also lent color to the Common. There was Granther Stannard, sea captain turned cobbler and self-taught dentist, who dwelled in a sod hut called "The Boo." And there was Sammy Markey, who had learned the homely arts of washing and ironing. He traveled from house to house with an apron tied at his waist and a shawl around his shoulders, the day's knitting protruding from his pocket. (He and the mannish Old Ruth would have made a strangely conventional married couple.) Like many others in the village, Sammy earned his keep by telling fortunes, his gleaned from coffee grounds.

Dogtown was also home to younger "witches" such as Moll Jakups and Judy Rhimes, who set their sights on males trekking down from Rockport or up from Gloucester. When the girls spied a likely prospect, they tied on their lace caps, tugged down their bodices, draped bare arms across open windows, and sang out: "Got a half-dollar, sailor? C'mon up!"

The most feared witch of Dogtown was a big brute of a woman named Tammy Younger, an obese creature with two walrus-like tusks thrusting from her upper jaw (the result of a botched tooth extraction by amateur dentist Granther Stannard). Tammy Younger and her sidekick, Aunt Luce George, together exhibited a special talent for detaining passing wagons: From a hundred paces they could send out the evil eye to stop a team of oxen in its tracks, the poor beasts standing stock still with tongues lolling. If a driver refused to surrender his pile of logs, crates of potatoes, or basin of fish, the two stout old hags could apparently, from that same hundred-foot distance, levitate the cargo clean off the back of the wagon.

But Tammy Younger's gruesomeness was part of her charm. Seamen and buccaneers sought her out in her lair to have their fortunes told between rounds of rum. When she died in her bed at the age of seventy-six, the still-terrorized community chipped in to appease her spirit with a silver-plated coffin. On the stormy night of her passing, the inmates of her house refused to retire to bed until Walrus-Tusk Tammy's casket was removed from the premises. On the following morning, the old witch was buried and a collective sigh of relief went up from the community.

In 1814, the last citizen of Dogtown was Black Neil Finson, a hobo who had done odd jobs for the witches in exchange for food and shelter. His aged benefactors died one by one, until he was left with nothing for company but the wind whistling through the six remaining houses. Like a hermit crab, Black Neil took up residence in one abandoned shell of a house after another until the rafters tumbled down on him. His favorite abode was Judy and Moll's old place, for he was convinced the long-dead prostitutes had laid up a treasure of gold in their cellar. When the roof caved in, he burrowed deeper, obsessively digging in the earthen floor for years on end. At last in 1830 the constable from Rockport, lured by rumors of an emaciated last survivor of Dogtown, traveled up to investigate. He found old Neil nearly frozen, filthy, starving, and clawing with scabrous hands at the floor of Moll and Judy's cellar. The constable conveyed Neil to Rockport's poorhouse, where the last Dogtowner died within a week. The postmortem report pronounced him "dead of sheer comfort."

In 1845 a work crew was sent up the Dogtown paths to pull down what remained of the derelict structures. Grass gradually filled in the footpaths, and wild roses, bayberry, and thistle seeded the abandoned yards. Oddly, a manmade feature was later added to the landscape: During the Great Depression a philanthropist named Roger Babson hired Finnish quarry workers to carve uplifting mottoes on the gigantic boulders. To this day, hikers in the area find their communion with nature augmented by exhortations to STUDY, USE YOUR HEAD, BE CLEAN, and HELP YOUR MOTHER, among other tips for healthy living. But there's another deeper, weirder experience for modern-day visitors when they arrive at this place on a chilly autumn afternoon. As they wander among the tall boulders, some have heard the shouts of dead buccaneers and the shrill cries of ancient fortune-tellers. After the voices die away, a spectral hush comes over the barren landscape, and there's a palpable sense, for those who know the history, that old Tammy Younger roams free of her silver-plated coffin.

Gloucester historian Thomas Dresser, author of *Dogtown, a Village Lost in Time,* wrote: "At first the abandoned inner Cape is uninviting. It seems remote and faintly forbidding. It retains the aura of a place that has seen both better times and sadder times. Perhaps ghost towns are an acquired taste—a mixture of peace and mystery and melancholy. The casual stroller often feels like a trespasser, if not in the legal sense, at least in the sense of intruding on a bereaved stranger."

╾ 23 ╼

Newburyport's Haunted Schoolhouse

About an hour's drive from Boston, at the northeastern tip of Massachusetts, the postcard-perfect town of Newburyport, birthplace of the U.S. Coast Guard, basks alongside the bay. In the commercial district, vintage brick-and-granite buildings have been gussied up for tourists. This brand of seaside adorableness also attracts its complement of artists, and thriving communities of theatre folk, painters, sculptors, and writers have burrowed into the quaint lanes of the town and along the open-sky shores, where estuaries and wild grasses meet in blue-and-green profusion.

But life in Newburyport wasn't quite so charming for the schoolchildren of 1870, forced to occupy the single-room structure at 32 Charles Street. It's hard enough to drum into students' brains that eight times eight equals sixty-four, and that the Battle of Hastings was fought in 1066, but when the drills are attempted over banging walls, ringing bells, stool-tappings, and indoor tornadoes, well, the teacher has her work cut out for her.

The little Cape-style building had beaten-up gray shingles and green blinds and was as run-down as any public schoolhouse of the time, with soiled doorposts, scratched floors, peeling paint, and a broken fence. When reports of eerie phenomena compelled the local school board to investigate the property, board members concluded that whatever was happening had been dredged up out of thin air. The all-boys school was a simple, bare, open classroom with sixty desks and a raised platform for the teacher. There were no niches, closets, mirrors, or objects outside the windows that might have cast frightening or misleading shadows. In other words, not only was there no place for ghosts to establish a covert field of operations, there was no place for a living perpetrator, such as a rude, disruptive schoolboy, to shelter himself in order to launch a battery of mystifying attacks.

But attacks there were aplenty. On an average day the disturbances began almost immediately as the boys recited their morning prayers. A deafening rap pounded the floors, climbed the walls, and galloped its way to the teacher's platform. Occasionally the knockings were loud enough to drown out the children's voices: the teacher would stare at moving lips, but no words were audible. Sometimes a series of raps assaulted the door. The first few times this event occurred, the teacher dutifully crossed to answer. No one was there. By the third or fourth time, she ignored the knocking.

The schoolmistress, Miss Lucy Perkins, was twenty-three years old, tall, tough, and courageous. It would take a lot more than a roomful of rambunctious spirits—human or inhuman—to rattle her. And it was a good thing she could take the haunting in stride; there were days when the commotion would have sent most people reeling into the surrounding fields.

A wood-burning stove warmed the open space before the students' desks. The stove lid had a wire handle that could be lifted with the help of a potholder. The poltergeist, or whatever invisible creature had charge of the stove, apparently required no buffer between the scalding metal and the appendage it deployed for fingers: sometimes the cast-iron lid levitated several inches above the burning coals, hung suspended in midair, then plopped back into place with a clatter.

The teacher had two bells on her desk, one bigger than the other. On many occasions an unseen hand grabbed the smaller bell, held it high, and clanged it vigorously as if calling the class to order. At times the circulation vent in the ceiling would be closed when it was supposed to be open, and vice versa, creating havoc with the climate in the room. The janitor, a sensible man and not by any means overimaginative, refused to enter the classroom without a companion for protection. In his words, "The noises are too much for me!"

Perhaps the eeriest feature of all was the play of light inside and outside the schoolhouse. Sometimes an unearthly golden glow permeated the classroom. On dark days it was seen to stream through a particular clerestory window. On stormy days the light could be discerned outdoors as well, emanating from walls as a shimmery aura. (It sounds almost angelic, but the other disruptions, obstreperous as they were, hinted at an unmistakably demonic presence.)

In addition, the schoolhouse was often under attack from powerful gusts of wind. On days when the town of Newburyport basked in calm air beside a placid sea, the little schoolhouse groaned and creaked under powerful gales that shook the wooden frames, almost as though a tiny, personal nor'-easter had been rustled up for the schoolhouse alone. Often the chimney pipe whistled as if a giant were blowing into it. In the grip of this barrage it was, of course, impossible for the pupils to focus on their lessons. They cast aside their primers as they stared around them with widening eyes. The stalwart Miss Perkins would sometimes instruct them to sing, presumably good Christian fighting hymns with verses such as "Furious they assailed us, but Thine Arms availed us / And Thy Word broke their swords, when our own strength failed us...." The students' high, sweet voices quavered against the *thrubs* and *drubs* of the poltergeist action.

It was lucky for Miss Perkins that the year was 1870 rather than 1670, when witch-phobic town elders would have blamed her for the whole sorry ordeal and hanged her from the nearest gallows (every Pilgrim village featured one). As it was, the redoubtable teacher was subjected to a thorough interrogation by the school authorities. The children as well were interviewed—bribed with sweets and threatened with corporal punishment—but they had nothing to reveal. Scary things happened in the school on Charles Street, and no one knew why or how to make them stop.

Although the school committee tried to keep these incidents a secret, word leaked out, as it invariably does, and soon regional newspapers picked up the story. While today, the haunting would be headlined by *20/20,* in those days sensational news items were written up as pamphlets and sold in shops and at newsstands. Loring of Boston published an account of the Newburyport schoolhouse story and sold it for twenty cents a copy (a nifty little treatise to be picked up today, should any copies still exist, in antiquarian bookstores).

No one in town in 1870, however, was profiting from the situation. Some of the townsfolk agitated to close the school. Others yearned to take things a step further and raze the building. Some parents removed their kids from school, but others stuck it out, since the school at 32 Charles Street offered the only education for miles around. By 1875 whatever had plagued the schoolhouse had packed up and gone on its merry way, with no definite plans, it was hoped, to infest another classroom elsewhere in the country. Many years ago the school was decommissioned and remodeled as a single-family dwelling. The family residing there today assures us that everything is quiet. Not quiet as the grave—we now suspect that's distinctly *un*quiet!—just quiet as in normal life.

⊰= 24 =⊱

A Buddy to Bartenders

An old photograph of Captain John Stone frowns above the bottles of booze lining the bar, his eyes darkly recessed under a shock of white hair. The wealthy sea captain, businessman, and landowner built the tavern in 1832 at 179 Main Street in Ashland, due west of Boston. A three-story building constructed of granite and chestnut was calculated to thrive beside the new railroad tracks running through town. And thrive it did. Captain Stone ran the Railroad Boarding House himself for a few years, then delegated the responsibility, and finally sold the business to his brother, Napoleon. Many owners succeeded the Stone brothers. One apparently had a clandestine operation going: some years back a secret room was discovered in the cellar, suggesting that the hotel was once a pit stop on the Underground Railroad, a place where runaway slaves could be hidden along the route to freedom.

For much of the twentieth century, the once-gracious lodge, renamed the Ashland Hotel, had deteriorated into a honky-tonk fogged with tobacco smoke and the smell of cheap beer. In the parking lot motorcycle gangs revved low-riding Harleys and smashed empty bottles on the asphalt before *thub-thub-thubb*ing away into the night. Then in 1972 a man named Leonard "Cappy" Fournier bought the historic building, endowed it with a major renovation, and, in a nod to its founder, christened it John Stone's Inn. Over the entrance these days, an Early American–style woodcut features the original owner's shock of white hair and grim black-eyed stare: Yes, the captain is back. In more ways than one.

Since the 1972 refurbishing, a Halloween bag of paranormal tricks and treats has spilled into the rooms. The highlight of these para-events is "that thing" with the tip jar: ten-dollar bills routinely show up without anyone knowing where they come from. In the 1980s bartender Eileen Streitenberger first reported arriving for the evening shift to find a ten-dollar bill awaiting her, even though she knew full well (and had it confirmed) that the day bartender had cleaned out the tip jar at the end of his shift. What's a girl to do but turn around and nod to the old fellow in the photograph behind her: "Thank you, John Stone."

Every worker at the inn has a story to relate. Cooks have encountered cans falling from counters when they weren't anywhere near the edge. Other employees, standing before the ice machine in the cellar, have felt their shoulders spectrally tapped—a favorite ghost "howdyado." Customers have taken photographs inside the lounge, then discovered on the prints nonexistent portraits shimmering on the walls behind the living subjects. Once a customer seated in the dining room felt two hands encircle her neck, squeezing hard. She managed to wheeze out the words, "Get my check!" Cappy Fournier was impressed that, even with a brutal entity choking the woman half to death, she managed to pay her bill.

With all the phantom tipping, shoulder tapping, and stranglings, only one visual apparition has graced the premises. This is a girl roughly nine years of age who shows up in the pantry off the kitchen. The cooks who've seen her early in the morning report that she turns from the window, smiles, and slowly fades away. One morning the first workers to arrive found the pantry window smashed, with the glass on the outside, indicating that the break had come from within. The inn had been fully locked the night before. There was no sign of a burglary or other mischief other than the shattered window.

Various mediums and even television crews have paraded through the inn to try to make sense of the chronic haunting. A psychic picked up a vibration that John Stone had once killed and buried in the cellar an itinerant salesman who cheated at cards. This led to random excavations in the cellar, but so far no bones have been recovered. Another medium intuited that money had been stolen from the slain salesman and stashed in a safe beneath the bar. This nougat of information intrigued Cappy Fournier, who, after he'd purchased the inn, had indeed discovered an antique safe under the counter. However, if a wad of cash had once been concealed there, some other enterprising innkeeper had stumbled upon it before him.

Bones in the basement? A brooding sea captain whose likeness still glowers misanthropically at present-day customers? Whatever is causing the chilly fingers of the supernatural to spread over the rooms of the John Stone Inn, any bartender there will assure you the mysterious ten-dollar tips make it all worth the bother.

⇒ 25 ⇒

Salem's Sad Legacy

The 1692 Salem Witchcraft Trials, which condemned to death twenty local townsfolk, are more than a disgraceful footnote in American history. And Salem is more than a tourist haunt where tens of thousands of annual visitors buy Gallows Hill mugs and pack the wax museum to view dungeon horrors reproduced in Colonial drag. Still, the Salem scandal was, and continues to be, in this writer's humble opinion, a seminal event in American culture that, in the post-traumatic shock it generated, stopped Puritanism in its extremist tracks and released its clerics' stranglehold on a fearful citizenry. In short, without Salem we might never have rid ourselves of our own Taliban.

The so-called witches of Salem, nineteen of whom hanged, and eighty-two-year-old Giles Corey, who was crushed to death under a multi-ton pile of rocks, had no sense of their immortal contribution to American freedom, yet today we might look on them as martyrs. The same stones that crushed Giles Corey in time reversed their mission, at least symbolically, and crushed Corey's persecutors in an equivalent tonnage of shame.

For, happily, a backlash followed the 1692 executions. It

took longer for witch hunting to die out completely—its "golden age" lasted from 1620 to 1725—but signs of remorse trickled in almost immediately, when one of the Salem judges, Samuel Sewall, publicly apologized for the part he'd played in the trials. Shortly thereafter the jury of Salem citizens also asked to be forgiven. And Cotton Mather, the most charismatic and ferocious of the judges, tainted by the growing stigma attached to the hangings, was rejected for the post of president of Harvard's Divinity School, even though as a churchman of the prestigious Mather line, he'd been groomed to follow in the footsteps of his father, Increase.

The final *coup de grace* to Puritanism was its own sudden disappearance. What happened to these churchmen, these dour forebears with their grim insistence that to smile in church on Sunday could get you flogged on Monday? Why have we no remaining dregs of that appalling belief structure? One can only speculate that sometime after the turn of the eighteenth century, every last Puritan, deeply embarrassed, must have packed his or her scarlet letters in drawers and slithered off to sign up at the local Quaker society or Unitarian fellowship or newfangled Methodist camp meeting. Whatever the case, thanks to the Salem Twenty, Puritanism in America is now as dead as dunking stools, white ruffled collars, and wooden pillories in town squares.

That said, a persistent psychic imprint of suffering hangs over Salem's streets and historic buildings. The gross injustice done to the accused by their neighbors is still being worked out in the form of ghostly payback. The last words of Giles Corey, for instance, have long been taken as a bona fide—and efficient—curse spanning the centuries. The reason rocks had been heaped on Corey's naked old body was that Puritan law enforcement had found this an ingenious way to squeeze confessions from otherwise mute prisoners. In the practice of the day, accused witches who pled not guilty were hanged, those who pled guilty were jailed and sometimes down the line hanged, so Mr. Corey, faced with these lousy choices, refused to speak, period. Finally, the evil Sheriff Corwin stood on the pile of stones crushing Corey to add still more weight. He bellowed down at his victim, "Do you confess?"

Corey croaked out, "Damn you, Sheriff. I curse you and Salem!"

For the next three hundred years, every high sheriff of Essex County, from the cruel George Corwin to friendly writer/ghost hunter/former sheriff Robert Cahill, has suffered from the Curse of Giles Corey. Sheriff Corwin was so universally reviled that when he died of a heart attack in 1696, his body was buried in his basement (now the extravagantly haunted Joshua Ward House) to prevent enraged townsfolk from digging up and defiling his corpse. As Cahill wrote in his 1992 book, *Haunted Happenings,* "All the high sheriffs of Essex County since Corwin, headquartered at the Salem Jail located in the field where Giles Corey was crushed to death, died in office from heart attack or were forced to retire because of heart conditions or blood ailments....When I [resigned] in 1978, it was after suffering a heart attack, stroke, and undergoing many blood transfusions for a rare blood disease. Were we all victims, I wonder, of Giles Corey's curse?"

True to the accused "warlock's" hex, Salem itself has endured more than its share of small-town tragedies, the most cataclysmic of which was the fire of 1914. The event was presaged by an inordinate number of Giles Corey sightings—a ghastly creature, all bones and tattered rags—in and near the Howard Street Burying Ground. This apparition had been reported for the past 222 years and was said to predict looming disaster. Even native son Nathaniel Hawthorne weighed in on the Giles Corey connection: "The ghost of the wizard appears as a precursor of some calamity impending over the community."

One-third of the maritime town was destroyed in the blaze that began, tellingly enough, at Gallows Hill, where the nineteen female victims had been hanged. Gale-force winds whipped the flames from one rooftop to the next, from the heart of town clear down to the shore, though, ironically, every last historic building was spared.

Some of these historic sites have, along with Giles Corey, cast a dark spell over the town. The original jail of 1692 had been torn down in 1812 to accommodate a new jail and the sheriff's house behind the cemetery. The dungeon below the old jail, where the accused were held and routinely tortured, was unearthed in 1957 when the phone company laid a new foundation. Several oak beams were recovered from the ancient holding pen and put on display at the Essex Institute and Salem's Witch Dungeon Museum.

The museum, with its reenactments of the hellish events of 1692, opened for business in 1979, and from its very inception was rife with hauntings. The young actresses who played the Colonial teens repeatedly fled the basement in hysterics when a rocking chair containing the mannequin of a hooded devil rocked itself. Each of the actresses, too, swore she'd seen a gray-robed spectre gliding among the creepy fixtures. The girls took to calling the phantom "the minister," which surprised local historians, for they alone knew that the museum had once been the site of a church.

But the main locus of Salem's hauntings is the Joshua Ward House, a Federal-style brick mansion built, as previously mentioned, on the foundation of Sheriff George Corwin's original abode and temporary place of burial. (F.Y.I.: George Washington slept in a second-floor guest room of the Joshua Ward House in 1789.) What failed to come to light, until a real estate broker named Richard Carlson purchased the property in 1981, was that the building housed an extremely nasty-looking ghost. The creature has been captured on Polaroid—a slim figure in a black tunic with an unruly nest of shoulder-length black hair and a malevolent expression on her otherwise indistinct but darkly complected face. After Richard Carlson and his agents set up shop, many of them would come to work in the morning to find their offices ransacked—waste baskets and lamps overturned, books and desk items scattered on the floor. In the first year of occupancy the fire alarm rang in the middle of the night on sixty separate occasions! Once, when a customer asked Carlson for a specific blueprint, a rolled-up plan wafted from the closet and unrolled itself on his desk—the exact specs that he needed.

But the ghost isn't always so helpful. At various times, in the room where George Washington once slept, people have reported a sensation of being throttled by unseen hands. It's hard to believe the spirit of our first president would behave in such a manner, so we'll rule him out as a suspect; but, interestingly, Sheriff George Corwin had relied on choking his prisoners to extract information. According to the testimony of condemned "warlock" John Proctor in 1692, the sheriff and his men had strangled the innocent sons of "witch" Martha Carrier: "The boys were tied neck and heels, 'till the blood was ready to come out their noses and eyes."

So we must add the Carrier boys to our roster of Salem martyrs. The evil done to them still hangs over the town, but the greater good for our country—the toppling of Puritan rule—enriches all of us.

PHOTO BY BETSY CONSIGLIA

Author and sometime ghost researcher Holly Nadler has written for television (*One Day at a Time, Laverne & Shirley, Barney Miller*, and others) and has published articles on a variety of topics in such magazines as *Cosmopolitan, Lear's, The Utne Reader, Woman's World, Cape Cod Life, Vineyard Style,* and *Martha's Vineyard Home & Garden*s.

Holly lives on Martha's Vineyard, in Oak Bluffs, where she recently opened a new bookstore, Sun Porch Books, and has for many years run a successful walking-tour business. Realizing that the most popular tour she has ever offered is "The Ghosts of Edgartown," Holly expanded on that theme to write *Haunted Island* (Down East Books, 1994), a collection of true ghost stories from the Vineyard.

Holly is also a regular visitor to Boston, where her city *pied-à-terre* is an Edwardian B&B on Beacon Hill.